How to Be a Philosopher

How to Be a Philosopher or How to Be Almost Certain that Almost Nothing is Certain

Gary Cox

BLOOMSBURY

LONDON • NEW DELHI • NEW YORK • SYDNEY

Bloomsbury Academic
An imprint of Bloomsbury Publishing Plc

50 Bedford Square
London
WC1B 3DP
UK

1385 Broadway
New York
NY 10018
USA

www.bloomsbury.com

BLOOMSBURY and the Diana logo are trademarks of Bloomsbury Publishing Plc

First published 2010, reprinted 2011

British Library Cataloguing-in-Publication Data
A catalogue record for this book is available from the British Library.

ISBN: HB: 978-1-44114-478-2
      PB: 978-1-47250-494-4
      ePDF: 978-1-44119-314-8
      ePub: 978-1-44117-481-9

Library of Congress Cataloging-in-Publication Data
A catalog record for this book is available from the Library of Congress.

Typeset by Newgen Knowledge Works (P) Ltd., Chennai, India
Printed and bound in Great Britain

For Mike

Contents

Introduction

Why have you started reading this book? Philosophers should avoid guessing, but my guess is that you already know a few things about philosophy and you want to know more. Or, at the very least, you have come across the word 'philosophy' before and you want to know what it means. Perhaps you already know a fair bit about philosophy – having studied it at college or university or in prison – but believe that knowing about philosophy and being a philosopher are very different things.

Philosophers, if I am one, should really avoid assuming anything, but on this occasion, instead of assuming that you, the reader, know something about philosophy, which you probably do, I'm going to force myself to assume that you know absolutely nothing about philosophy. You have lived on this earth for however long, you are intelligent enough and have become educated enough to be able to read this book. More to the point, you *want* to read this book; a remarkable thing in itself in an age when ignorance is the new intelligence. Nonetheless, the meaning and significance of philosophy totally passed you by like the proverbial ship in the night. You have heard of psychology and sociology, even physiology, psychiatry and philately, but philosophy just got overlooked somehow, like a city you've never visited though you are well travelled, like a visitor who called at your door during the 5 short minutes you were in the shower.

Philosophy has a reputation for being complicated. Mostly this reputation is undeserved although it is true that it can get very, very complicated at the most advanced levels. Philosophy can get more complicated than anything else in life in fact. More complicated than relationships, more complicated than taxation, more complicated even than cricket. (As with cricket, many long, titanic struggles in philosophy end in draws.) Philosophy can get so complicated that it makes rocket science look like . . . well . . . not rocket science. Philosophy at an advanced level definitely *is* rocket science, although it has nothing whatsoever to do with designing vehicles that are capable of overcoming earth's gravitational pull or landing tiny probes on Mars by remote control at a distance of 55–400 million miles. Do not, however, be put off by all this talk of complexity. You will be relieved to know that being a philosopher, at least at a basic level, is actually incredibly simple. It really is, as this book will show.

Philosophy is a vast body of arguments, a great network of different points of view, a huge tangle of thorny issues that is still growing and expanding after thousands of years like unchecked brambles on a badly tended allotment. It would take many lifetimes to read all that has been written in philosophy, so not even the greatest philosophers know all the arguments. My point, however, is that to be a philosopher you don't actually have to know *any* of the arguments! Philosophy, as some great philosophers have said, is not so much a body of knowledge as an *activity*. So all you have to do to be a philosopher, at least at a basic level, is simply start *doing* philosophy; simply start *philosophizing*. It's a bit like playing tennis. You don't have to play tennis like Roger Federer or Rafael Nadal to be playing tennis. You are playing tennis, after a fashion, if you simply pick up a tennis racket and knock a couple of balls over the net, or even down into it.

It is almost certain that you have philosophized a fair amount in your life already without realizing it. In that case, you are already a philosopher without knowing it. If you have ever wondered where the universe comes from or if there is anything after you die, if you know anything for sure or if life is totally meaningless, if there is any good reason why you should be morally good or even bad or if beauty is simply in the eye of the beholder, then you were doing philosophy. The big irony for me is that I'm writing this book to tell people how to become something they almost certainly are already! I'm preaching to the converted, teaching my grandmother to suck eggs, taking coals to Newcastle and oil to Texas. So maybe the title of this book should be *How to Tell When you are Doing Philosophy* or, sounds a bit pretentious, *How to Philosophize More Effectively*.

The plain truth of the matter, without wanting to disrespect anyone, is that most of the very basic philosophizing that people do at the bus stop or in the pub or in their head while lying in bed unable to sleep has already been done far more thoroughly by someone who did nothing else but obsess over that particular speck of philosophizing for their entire, miserable life. So much so in some cases that they never had time to catch a bus or go to the pub or even sleep. I dare to say this as I have taught philosophy to hundreds of intelligent and not so intelligent beginners of all ages and rarely have any of them ever come up with an argument that someone, somewhere, sometime, didn't already write a whole book on or even a whole series of books.

As a philosophy teacher I have learnt to sit patiently and approvingly while a philosophy student offers me a well-worn argument that is documented *ad nauseam* in the great dusty annals that comprise the history of philosophy, as though his or her well-worn argument were a profoundly original insight. Of course, for the student, it is a profoundly original insight and greatly to be encouraged, hence my approving patience. But as there is no point reinventing the wheel and philosophy courses wouldn't make much progress if they did nothing else but reinvent the wheel, I eventually shoot the student down in flames by pointing out that the great philosopher Descartes, or whoever it was, already said whatever it was hundreds of years ago and in a lot more detail. Actually, the student is not usually too downhearted as it flatters their ego to think that they came up with the same point as the great Descartes. It's a bit like flattering someone with the thought that they just played the same kind of masterful backhand volley as Federer played in the Wimbledon men's singles final of 2009.

Surely, nobody plays tennis with the intention of getting worse, so wanting to play tennis is wanting to be better at tennis even if you know you'll never be as good as Federer or Nadal or even Henman. (To be fair, Henman was the best player in Britain for years and fourth best in the world at one time. Pretty damned good really.) Usually, wanting to be a philosopher is wanting to be better at it even if you know you'll never be as good as David Hume or Immanuel Kant – two of the biggest all-time hitters in the age-old game of philosophy. Knowing some of the tried and trusted procedures of the age-old philosophy game, some of the main positions in its vast body of well-worn arguments and some of the main twisted strands in its great point-of-view network, will certainly help you to be a more effective philosopher. A philosopher who can hit balls over the net rather than just down into it, a philosopher who can serve and return service, maybe even a philosopher who can sometimes win game, set and match against a worthy opponent who has been practicing too.

The basics of philosophy are relatively easy to grasp and so it is easy to play the philosophy game at a relatively decent level, enough to enjoy it, enough to spar with almost anyone who isn't an Oxbridge professor of philosophy. In case you don't know, Oxbridge is a mythical university that is either Oxford or Cambridge or both. It is not a place midway between Oxford and Cambridge – that title goes roughly to Milton Keynes or Luton.

To be a really great philosopher, however, now that's really tough. Maybe harder even than winning Wimbledon. Plato, Aristotle, Hume, Kant, Hegel, Mill, Kierkegaard, Wittgenstein, Sartre, de Beauvoir – these great philosophers dedicated their whole life to philosophy, racking their considerable brainy heads day after day, year in and year out, decade after decade, vast heavy book after vast heavy book. The great philosophers are like huge mountains in the vast terrain of philosophy, whereas someone like me, for example, who teaches philosophy and has written a few commentaries (books *about* great philosophers) is a mere molehill. But not to worry. Philosophers great and small, from Plato's Everest down to Rab C. Nesbitt's hillock, know that size is relative and that it's better to be a small mound of philosophy than a large pit of ignorance. We will look at some of the outstanding features of those huge mountains of philosophy as we go, some of the key ideas of the great philosophers that have cast such long shadows of influence over human thought and progress.

So, where are we? Even if you have never heard of philosophy until now and still don't really know what the word *philosophy* means, it is nonetheless highly probable that you have philosophized many times in your life already without realizing that what you were doing was called *philosophizing* and that the sum total of humankind's accumulated and still accumulating philosophizing is called *philosophy*. If you have philosophized at all, just a tad, and haven't made a deliberate decision to *avoid* doing anything so seemingly pointless and potentially disturbing again, then you are already a philosopher. And if you are already a philosopher then it follows that you don't need to be told how to be a philosopher. Can you tell someone who already rides a bicycle how to ride a bicycle?

Well, it depends what you mean by riding a bicycle. By the way, saying 'it depends what you mean' is central to the activity of philosophy. Anyone who *really* knows how to ride a bike – seven times Tour de France winner, Lance Armstrong, for example – will tell you that there is riding a bike and riding a bike. At one level, there is staying upright and making progress and stopping without falling off; then at another level there is rider position, efficient use of gears, cadence, cornering, controlled braking, drafting, zipping your shirt up with both hands just before you start descending and a thousand other little skills to boot that make up *really* knowing how to ride a bicycle.

So perhaps this book shouldn't simply be called *How to be a Philosopher* – although that's obviously the catchy sounding title the marketing people and I decided to stick with – but *How to **Really** be a Philosopher* or *How to be a **Better** Philosopher*. In a sense, these alternative titles I keep rather tediously suggesting are *all* the subtitles of this little book but they were too dull or too long for the front or even the back cover.

I'm no Lance Armstrong but I have done a lot of cycling in my life. I'm no Aristotle but I have done a lot of philosophizing in my life, largely because I somehow fell into the ridiculous practice of trying to scrape a living at it. It has kept a somewhat leaky roof over my head but there is a lot more money in margarine I assure you. I believe, therefore, I can give you a few pointers on how to peddle your philosophy bicycle a bit faster without getting saddle sore or skidding off the road into some of the main pit falls and ditches.

It is important to mention, by way of concluding this introduction, that being a philosopher has both advantages and disadvantages. Trained philosophers tend to think, write and argue more coherently than ordinary folk. They have acquired the art of joined up thinking and talking. This is a great advantage when it comes to getting and keeping those jobs that tend to be the most secure, interesting and well paid. Research has shown that people with qualifications in philosophy, far from being a bunch of dropouts, tend to do very well when it comes to training to be teachers, lawyers, doctors, computer scientists, marketing strategists, journalists and even plumbers. This is because, in studying philosophy, people study the basic principles of all knowledge. Studying philosophy gives a person the ultimate transferable skill set. If you can learn to read the famously complicated German philosopher, Martin Heidegger, for example, then the explanatory notes to your next tax form will read like Enid Blyton. I will return to the theme of the professional advantages of studying philosophy in the final chapter.

Of course, all this ability to think and argue coherently that the philosopher has is equally likely to cause offence amongst ordinary, unthinking folk whose heads are full of fluff. When the philosopher ties them in knots simply by pointing out the inconsistencies and confusions in their absurd point of view, they will label him a smart arse and are likely to start plotting his downfall. This is exactly what happened to the ancient Greek philosopher, Socrates. He publicly humiliated so many powerful Athenians by showing them that they didn't know their arse from their elbow that they eventually forced him to drink the deadly poison, hemlock.

It is unlikely in this day and age that however much of a smart arse you are you will be forced to drink hemlock. Thanks to our mass-media culture, smart arses are now ten a penny. If the average loudmouthed, opinionated TV presenter hasn't been forced to drink hemlock then you've probably got nothing to worry about. Does anyone even know how to make hemlock anymore?

Philosophers often rub people up the wrong way with their finely tuned ability to touch a nerve or deliver a home truth right into the jugular, but generally they manage to avoid execution by realizing in their infinite wisdom that discretion is the better part of valour. In other words, they leg it to another town or country, adding exile to their list of achievements. Often they flee to the Netherlands where mind-altering ideas have always been as tolerated by the liberal authorities there as mind-altering substances. Even Socrates could have fled ancient Athens, apparently, but he was determined to be a martyr and insisted that death held no fear for him. On being condemned to death, he coolly said:

> Death is one of two things. Either it is annihilation, and the dead have no consciousness of anything; or, as we are told, it is really a change: a migration of the soul from this place to another. Now if there is no consciousness but only a dreamless sleep, death must be a marvellous gain. (*Apology*, 39d)

A far more immediate threat to the philosopher than execution is the slide into *nihilism*. Nihilism is belief in nothing to the point of despair. Studying philosophy might lead you, as it did Socrates, to the conclusion that there are higher powers and other dimensions giving life an ultimate meaning and purpose. Alternatively, it might well leave you struggling to make sense of the very notion of *ultimate* meaning and purpose. There is always the danger that it will lead you to the crushing conclusion that life is so ultimately meaningless and pointless that it is totally and utterly absurd. Not just absurd in parts – stamp collecting, amusing ring tones, soap operas, wearing a tie, moustaches – but absurd as a whole.

Actually, deciding that life is totally and utterly absurd need not lead to despair. Many philosophers who have reached the nihilistic philosophical position that life is totally and utterly absurd have quickly gone on to clinch victory from the jaws of defeat, declaring that if life is totally and utterly absurd and has no meaning *in itself*, then each individual life must have the meaning each person chooses to give it. This anti-nihilistic position, held by such *existentialist* philosophers as Friedrich Nietzsche and Jean-Paul Sartre, is not only supposed to be positive but hugely empowering on a personal level. Not least, it clears all that oppressive religious stuff out of the way and makes a person the master or mistress of his or her own destiny.

The philosopher Arthur Schopenhauer decided that God does not exist. 'God is dead' is how Nietzsche later put it, meaning that for intelligent people the *idea* of God is obsolete as an explanation for how things are. This led Schopenhauer to the despairing conclusion that life, the universe and everything must be meaningless if there is no God to give it meaning. This is as far as he got philosophically, plunged deep in what is now known as *Schopenhauerian nihilism*. Away from his books, however, he remained quite a cheerful fellow, was a loving father to his children and played the flute every morning. Anyway, his successor Nietzsche came along and said, in so many words, hold on, this 'God is dead' business need not be a cause for despair after all. In fact, it should be a cause for celebration because it means there is no boss, that the way ahead is open and unlimited, that we are free to create all the meanings and values in the universe and so be gods ourselves. In a book called *The Gay Science* – that's 'gay' in the older sense of the word – Nietzsche wrote:

> Indeed, we philosophers and 'free spirits' feel, when we hear the news that 'the old god is dead' as if a new dawn shone on us; our heart overflows with gratitude, amazement, premonitions, expectation. At long last the horizon appears free to us again, even if it should not be bright; at long last our ships may venture out again, venture out to face any danger; all the daring of the lover of knowledge is permitted again; the sea, *our* sea, lies open again; perhaps there has never yet been such an 'open sea'. (*Gay Science*, 343, p. 280)

This is bold, stirring, rebellious stuff from Nietzsche, but it is hard not to sympathize with the wise old saying that there are no atheists in a battle trench when the bullets start flying. This, of course, doesn't prove that God exists, only that despite what Nietzsche says, despite all his audacious atheism, there are extreme occasions when the need to believe in some kind of god is pretty much overwhelming, unless you have become a god yourself of course. So many lifelong non-believers, gripped by pain and fear of the unknown, pray with their last breath. Do they suddenly genuinely believe or are they just playing it safe by attempting to whisper a few humble, beseeching words in God's ear just in case he exists after all? I don't know the answer to this question and if I ever find it I'll probably be too busy praying with my last gasp to tell anyone. All I can say is they definitely want to believe. All that aside, theist or atheist, a true philosopher should always strive to avoid believing things just because they sooth his fears or satisfy his desires. He should always seek the truth without compromise, for its own sake, as the ultimate prize, whatever the truth may turn out to be.

If philosophy is a hard headed, no nonsense, uncompromising search for the truth then to be a philosopher you have to go where the search takes you, not where your softer, more sentimental side would like to go. The poet John Keats once wrote, 'Do not all charms fly at the mere touch of cold philosophy? . . . Philosophy will clip an Angel's wings, Conquer all mysteries by rule and line, Empty the haunted air, and gnomed mine – Unweave a rainbow' (*Lamia*: Part II, 229, in *The Complete Poems of John Keats*). Perhaps the great poet, who was actually a bit of a philosopher as well, is getting a little carried away here, as poets do, in stressing how philosophy tends to put a dampener on life by taking the mystery out of it. After all, some philosophy is as good as poetry at instilling a sense of awe and wonder in the sublime beauty and awesome complexity of the universe. Nonetheless, I have to admit that Keats has a point, not least because philosophy wants to get to the bottom of mysteries, clear the air of phantoms and confusions and march all those silly gnomes out of the cave of ignorance up into the clear light of reason.

Studying philosophy, becoming a philosopher, is not a neutral process. It will change the way you think and feel about your life, possibly for the better, possibly not. It might give you faith in something higher or destroy your faith in everything. I don't know. Anyway, you have been warned. Read on if you dare.

1 What is Philosophy?

When learning how to be a philosopher, or how to be a better philosopher, it certainly helps to know what philosophy is. I've already said a few things about what philosophy is in the Introduction, namely, that it is the sum total of humankind's accumulated and still accumulating philosophizing. Now, philosophers have turned their philosophical eye, their powers of reason and logic, upon all the philosophizing that has been done down through the centuries and in doing so have identified certain recurrent themes and patterns in philosophy and drawn certain conclusions about them. There is no area of life or human practice that philosophers don't scrutinize and analyse with their precise, unbiased judgement. Hence, there are philosophies of science, maths, politics, history, education, psychology, law, emotion, sex, even football. It is not surprising then that there is also a philosophy of philosophy, that philosophers have philosophized since ancient times about what philosophy is. Like most people, philosophers can be pretty self-obsessed. This book is itself just another small contribution to that self-obsessed debate. In short, 'What is philosophy?' is itself an interesting, age-old philosophical question to which various answers have been given.

Like most philosophical questions there is no final right or wrong answer to the question, 'What is philosophy?', certainly not one that all philosophers agree upon, but there are better and worse answers. Someone who is familiar with philosophy as a subject and a practice has no difficulty understanding what philosophy is and what it is not. The difficulty lies in *summarizing* what it is. We all know what maths is, but imagine how difficult it would be to summarize what maths is to someone who had never come across it before.

Philosophy and defining

One thing that can be said with confidence about philosophy is that it aims to eliminate confusion about what we mean by the words we use. It searches for accurate *definitions*, accurate statements that state the essential properties of things. I drive my philosophy students mad with the whole business of definition and they drive me mad with their resistance to seeing how important definition is. I constantly pester them to define words and terms accurately, to come up with definitions that are so specific to the thing being defined that they couldn't possibly apply to anything else. That is what a definition is or should be. It captures the essence of something.

Before I have drilled them like an ill-tempered sergeant-major in the importance of accurate definitions, my students, if they don't just offer the class an *example* of a type of thing, tend to offer the class a statement that could apply equally to several different types of thing rather than an accurate, exclusive definition that picks out just one type of thing. For example, if I ask a novice student to define 'murder' he might well reply, 'Murder is, like, well, you know, when someone gets killed.' This answer is obviously on the right track because it mentions killing and it doesn't mention that murder is a two legged creature with feathers and wings, but it is not a definition of 'murder' because not every instance of someone getting killed is an instance of murder, even if every murder involves someone getting killed.

We have wonderful A–Z collections of definitions called dictionaries. According to my faithful, dog-eared old copy of *The New Collins Concise English Dictionary* the definition of 'murder' is 'the unlawful premeditated killing of one human being by another'. Hopefully, you can see how this statement, this *definition*, really captures the essence of what murder is as distinct from the essence of manslaughter or death by misadventure or the price of bread or skiing or paper clips or any other kind of thing in the world.

The ancient Greek philosopher, Aristotle, set out to find the definition of 'man'. 'Two legged creature', he recognized, wouldn't work, as there are other kinds of two legged creature in the world, most notably birds. 'Featherless biped' he suggested. This was better as it excluded the birds and picked out man as the only kind of creature, certainly that Aristotle knew of, that is both two legged and non-feathered. Then again, an oven-ready chicken is two legged and non-feathered but that doesn't make it a human being. Possibly with this kind of culinary thought in mind, Aristotle finally went for 'Man is a rational animal' as the best definition of 'man' because human beings are the only things in the world that are both animals and rational.

Noting that human beings are often far from rational in the way they think and behave, Jonathan Swift, the seventeenth-century satirist, most famous for writing *Gulliver's Travels*, altered Aristotle's definition to 'Man is an animal *capable* of reason.' More recently, some philosophers, particularly those interested in the issue of animal rights, have argued that some non-human animals are also rational. If they are, then Aristotle's classic definition of 'man' is undermined, which just goes to show how hard it is to be certain you have really defined a thing.

Defining 'philosophy'

'Where is all this leading?' I hear you cry. He was just about to tell us what philosophy is when he started banging on about definition, his poor hard-pressed students and some Greek geezer called Aristotle. Well, apart from the fact that understanding definition is an important part of understanding what philosophy is and how it works, I wanted to set the scene for talking about the *definition* of the term 'philosophy' itself. In searching for the definition of the term 'philosophy' we can do no better than look at what the dictionary says. After all, dictionaries are written by people who fall into that line of work because they are particularly good at defining things. Moreover, they build on the efforts of generations of lexicographers (as dictionary writers are known) who have been creating and refining definitions since the time of Dr Samuel 'Dictionary' Johnson – the man who completed the awesome task of writing the first proper English dictionary in 1755.

The first thing you notice when you look up 'philosophy' in a dictionary, apart from the word itself of course, is that there are a number of related definitions referring to different *uses* of the word. The fact that the same word is often used in different ways poses huge problems for the whole business of accurate definitions that are supposed to capture the essential properties of a thing, problems that have spawned whole branches of the philosophy of language.

Many modern philosophers, most notably the great twentieth-century Austrian philosopher, Ludwig Wittgenstein, argue that definitions are artificial and the search for them misguided. Philosophers, he argues, should investigate the *use* of words rather than their definitions if they want to make any real progress in philosophy. I have a lot of sympathy with what Wittgenstein is saying but I won't go into my reasons now. Wittgenstein is rather advanced stuff and if we get drawn off down that particular winding track we may never get back to the broad beginners' highway we are following at the moment. Philosophers question and criticize everything, and definitions are no exception. Nonetheless, it is useful to the process of beginning to understand what philosophy is to look at the various related definitions of the word as presented in a dictionary.

My faithful, much used, dog-eared old dictionary gives the following set of definitions of the word 'philosophy':

philosophy:

1. The rational investigation of being, knowledge and right conduct.
2. A system or school of thought: for example, *the philosophy of Descartes*.
3. The basic principles of a discipline: for example, *the philosophy of law*.
4. Any system of beliefs, values, or tenets.
5. A personal outlook or viewpoint.
6. *Philosophical.* Serenity of temper.

I won't comment directly on this set of definitions, not least because they speak pretty well for themselves, but I might refer back to them once or twice as we go, so keep them in mind, or at least remember the number of the page so you can flick back to it quickly.

What the dictionary also adds in a squiggly bit at the end of the entry which deals with *etymology* (word history) is that the word 'philosophy' itself is derived from 'philos', the Greek word for 'love', and 'sophia', the Greek word for 'wisdom'. So, literally speaking, philosophy is love of wisdom and a philosopher is a lover of wisdom. Without further ado I can say with more certainty than is often possible in philosophy that if you want to be a philosopher then you must become a lover of wisdom, knowledge and truth for their own sake. I already said as much or nearly as much in the Introduction when I said that a philosopher should always seek the truth for its own sake and avoid believing things just because they satisfy his softer, more sentimental side.

If you are at all observant – some people are not observant at all – you will have noticed that in everyday life the words 'philosophy' and 'philosophical' are used by a wide variety of people in a wide variety of situations to mean a wide variety of different things. For example, you have probably heard a hippie-type person at Glastonbury Festival or the Stonehenge Solstice Gathering say, 'My philosophy is not to worry about anything, man.' Whereas you have probably heard a ruthless business tycoon-type person on the Bloomberg Channel say, 'The philosophy of my multinational company is to maximize profit at every opportunity.' As for 'philosophical', this is a word often used to describe a person who does not regret anything (perhaps he does not hope for anything either) and always says, 'Oh well, that's life' when anything goes wrong. He is wise enough to be philosophical about things going wrong because he has learnt, perhaps from bitter personal experience, that in life things tend to go wrong despite all efforts to the contrary and that there is really no use crying over spilt milk or even spilt limbs.

I'm reminded of the English gentleman officer in the Monty Python film, *The Meaning of Life,* who is totally unfazed at having his leg bitten off by a tiger. 'Woke up just now, one sock too many,' he says casually. When asked how it feels he simply replies, 'Stings a bit.' This courageous impassivity and resignation in face of adversity, this preserving of a stiff upper lip, once so valued by the English ruling classes in general and the English public schools in particular, is called *stoicism* and people who have it are described as stoic or stoical. The Stoics were a group of long-suffering ancient Greek philosophers who held that happiness can only be achieved by submitting to destiny, accepting that in life 'shit happens' and adopting an attitude of complete indifference to pleasure and pain.

There is nothing wrong with the common or everyday uses of the words 'philosophy' and 'philosophical'. There are no word-police to say that people can't use these words in these ways if they want to. Nevertheless, these uses are vague. In the first two examples, the word 'philosophy' adds nothing more to the meaning of the sentences in which it is used than would the words 'approach', 'attitude' or 'aim'. However, there may be a deeper purpose behind the use of the word 'philosophy' on the part of the hippie or the tycoon. Namely, to indicate that their so-called philosophy is the product of thought and consideration. Suppose that after much marijuana-clouded contemplation the hippie decides that nothing matters except not worrying, while after much cold-blooded mental calculation the tycoon concludes that nothing matters except financial profit. Well, such *processes* of thought and consideration are closer to what should be understood by the term 'philosophy'.

Philosophy, strictly speaking, is not so much to do with the attitudes, beliefs, views, values and opinions that people happen to have, but rather with the *reasoning,* or *lack of reasoning* behind people's attitudes, beliefs, views, values and opinions. Philosophy students often ask me, when worrying about what to write in their philosophy essays and exams, 'Can I put my own opinions?' The answer I tend to give to this question is that you can put your own opinions, but it doesn't really matter whether or not they are in fact *your* opinions. What matters are the reasons and arguments you give to support whatever claims you make. A person's beliefs and opinions, if he or she wants to be a genuine philosopher, should always be arrived at via a process of sound, unbiased, objective reasoning. Seldom is it the case of course that people arrive at their beliefs and opinions through sound, unbiased, objective reasoning. If they did, there wouldn't be so many woolly brained, half-baked, biased, subjective, unreasonable notions endlessly circling the globe and causing so much trouble. I fear to draw up a specific list for you as the world's most half-baked and unreasonable dogmas, unable to defend themselves against criticism using reason, often resort to defending themselves against criticism using threats and violence.

On the basis of all that has been said so far, it seems that we are ready to assert the following 3 things about the nature of philosophy:

1. *Philosophy is an activity* that exposes falsehoods, inconsistencies and absurdities in various points of view with the aim of discovering the truth.
2. *Philosophy uses reason* – in practice, reasoned argument – to expose these falsehoods, inconsistencies and absurdities. The cutting edge of reason is *logic.* I'll say more about logic in a moment.
3. *Philosophy involves thinking about all sides of an argument or debate.* It requires freedom of thought and expression and

philosophers are – or should be – encouraged to think and speak freely without fear of seeming foolish or politically incorrect. I'll say more about freedom of thought and expression shortly.

Philosophy and cold, hard logic

As said, the cutting edge of reason is *logic*. Remember Mr Spock in *Star Trek*, he of the pointy ears. Spock is a good man (or rather Vulcan) to have around in a crisis because his thinking is always perfectly clear and logical. What is more, he is never slow to point out when someone else's thinking is confused and illogical. 'That's illogical Captain' is virtually his catch phrase, the line everyone uses when attempting to impersonate him. Cold, hard logic is the cutting edge of reason because rational thinking is logical thinking; thinking that avoids making unjustified assumptions as it advances through clear, logical steps that follow necessarily from one another. Logic can get very complicated and there is a whole branch of philosophy called *formal logic* that studies logic for its own sake, but, very basically, logic involves deducing conclusions from premises and identifying contradictions, or the lack of them, in beliefs and arguments.

The easiest way to explain deducing conclusions from premises is with an age-old example. Consider the following simple logical argument called a *syllogism* in which the two premises necessarily imply the conclusion:

First Premise: All men are mortal.
Second Premise: Socrates is a man.
Conclusion: Therefore, Socrates is mortal.

Given the premises, we can see that the conclusion follows *logically* from them. We say the premises *imply* or *entail* the conclusion. If all members of a certain set of things is mortal then any particular member of that set of things must also be mortal. Socrates belongs to the set of all men because he too is a man so he absolutely must be mortal. I'm probably insulting your intelligence by labouring the point. You've probably got it already, but if you haven't, just think about it some more and it will click. After all, you are a rational animal, as Aristotle says, and are therefore uniquely well placed to recognize the self-evident logic of the above syllogism. By the way, it was Aristotle who invented the syllogism. Yet another of his many achievements in philosophy and science.

In the next example, although both premises and the conclusion are each true in themselves, the premises do not logically *imply* the conclusion. This argument, as I hope you can see, is not logical.

First premise:	Plato is mortal.
Second premise:	Socrates is a man.
Conclusion:	Therefore, Socrates is mortal.

You can't know, simply from knowing that Plato is mortal and Socrates is a man that Socrates too is mortal. To get a little bit technical for a moment, for the syllogism to be logical the first premise needs to make a *universal* claim about all members of a set to which Socrates belongs, but it only makes a claim about a *particular* thing, namely Plato. Plato, by the way, was not Aristotle's or Socrates' dog but an extremely important ancient Greek philosopher in his own right. Much more about Plato shortly.

A final syllogism for you to think about:

First premise:	All pigs are sheep.
Second premise:	All sheep are goats.
Conclusion:	Therefore, All pigs are goats.

Surprisingly, although the premises and the conclusion are absurd, this argument is logical because the premises necessarily imply the conclusion. We know from experience that pigs are not sheep and that sheep are not goats and so on, but *IF* we suppose for argument's sake that they are, as this argument does, then the conclusion logically follows.

'*IF* all pigs are sheep and *IF* all sheep are goats then . . .'. As a professor of philosophy once said to me during my first ever philosophy lesson, 'IF is a very big word in philosophy.' To get a bit technical again for a moment, what matters here is the *form* or structure of the argument rather than its *content*. The form is logical even though the content is absurd. Rather than possibly confusing you with pigs, sheep and goats it would have been better to do away with the content of the argument and instead emphasize its form simply by saying, 'If all *a* is *b* and all *b* is *c* then all *a* is *c*.'

As said, logic also involves recognizing contradictions, or the lack of them, in beliefs and arguments. There is nothing like seizing on a contradiction to show a person he doesn't know what the hell he is talking about, but what exactly is a contradiction? A person contradicts himself when there is a lack of consistency in what he says. Often a person contradicts himself when he is lying because he is struggling to make all the pieces of a made-up story fit together, as well as fit the known facts. For example, a suspect might say, 'I don't drink alcohol,' and later on say, 'I was too drunk to remember what happened.' Even the worst liars usually have their stories better worked out than this, but you get the point. Detectives have to be particularly good at sniffing out far less obvious contradictions when they question suspects. Detecting a contradiction is often the first step towards cracking a guilty suspect's fabrications in order to get at the truth.

Of course, a person doesn't have to lie to contradict himself. Sometimes a person contradicts himself simply because he hasn't sufficiently thought through what he is saying to recognize that what he is saying is not consistent. We all do this from time to time because it is very hard, if not impossible, to monitor the consistency of everything we think and say.

Incidentally, don't you just hate it when you politely point out to someone who obviously isn't lying to you, someone who isn't *deliberately* attempting to mislead you, that he has just contradicted himself and he replies indignantly, 'Don't you call me a liar!' Generally, it is not worth dignifying this silly, defensive exclamation with a response. If you say, 'I'm not calling you a *liar*,' the person will simply assume you have conceded that what he said was not actually inconsistent after all!

The more of a philosopher you become the more you will notice the almost total lack of logic and reason with which many people speak and act. And the more you notice it, especially if you can't resist pointing it out, the more of a smart-arsed know-all some people will think you are. Beware they don't wreak their revenge on you. They are, after all, people ruled by sentiment who act first and think later, if they think at all. If you are truly wise then you will realize that sometimes the wisest thing to do in some situations is keep you mouth shut and live to fight another day.

Anyway, consider the following statement from an excellent book called *Logic* by the famous logician, Wilfrid Hodges: 'I have invented an amazing new sedative which makes people faster and more excited' (*Logic*, p. 15). As Hodges notes, the belief being expressed is inconsistent and the statement is self-contradictory as there is 'no possible situation in which a thing that made people faster and more excited could also be a sedative' (*Logic*, p. 15). *Alcohol, dose dependent.*

Although absurd claims are often self-contradictory it is important to note that a person can make an absurd claim without contradicting himself. Suppose a person seriously claimed that the moon is made of cheese. There is no contradiction involved here and to show the person that he is mistaken we would have to challenge his lack of experience – his lack of what is called *empirical knowledge* – rather than his lack of logic. We would have to convince him that men have been to the moon and found it to be made of rock and dust. That cheese and heavenly bodies have very different origins and that it is therefore *physically impossible* for the moon to be made of cheese.

Interestingly, it is not *logically impossible* for the moon to be made of cheese. It is possible to imagine a moon made of cheese and a moon made of cheese would not defy the laws of logic. On the other hand, the logically impossible, contradictory situation of a bachelor being a married man *would* defy the laws of logic. The statement or proposition, 'A bachelor is a married man,' is a good, standard example of a contradiction. Nothing and nobody can defy the laws of logic, perhaps not even God.

Without getting too deep into the issue it is worth bearing in mind that philosophers distinguish between two different types of possibility: *physical* or *empirical* possibility on the one hand, and *logical* possibility on the other. Science investigates the first type of possibility, philosophy and logic investigate the second type of possibility. I like to shock my students early on in philosophy courses by telling them it is logically possible to jump to the moon! They take me to be saying that a person can jump to the moon. When the ensuing outrage has subsided I'm able to draw the important distinction between empirical and logical possibility and point out that although it is empirically impossible for a person to jump to the moon, it is not logically impossible.

Identifying contradictions is one of our most fundamental means of understanding the world; so fundamental and obvious it hardly seems to need explaining. But precisely because it is so fundamental and obvious its significance is often overlooked. Although most of us have a good nose when it comes to sniffing out contradictions in the things other people say, we all frequently contradict ourselves without realizing we have done so. A good philosopher has to be as good at avoiding contradictions in the things he says as he is at identifying contradictions in the things other people say.

It was by leading people to contradict themselves when they attempted to explain their confused views that Socrates exposed the absurdity of many of the commonly held beliefs of the most important citizens of ancient Athens. Socrates practised what has come to be known as *Socratic method*. By asking polite question and pretending ignorance Socrates tempted people into a state of overconfidence in which they began to self-importantly spout their less than consistent views. Then, suddenly, he would hit them from below with an apparently innocuous question that they just couldn't answer one way or another without contradicting claims they had made with total conviction earlier in the conversation. He soon unravelled their argument and reduced their point of view to absurdity (*reductio ad absurdum*). Most of us use Socratic method ourselves at times in arguments with other people as a way of trying to catch them out and get the better of them. There are also numerous examples of it in books and films, especially court room dramas and detective stories.

The 1970s American TV detective, Lieutenant Columbo, played by Peter Falk, is a master at the art of Socratic method. Columbo questions a suspect while pretending to be a bit stupid. He scratches his head, witters on about his wife and fiddles in the pockets of his old beige rain mack as though his mind is elsewhere. The suspect relaxes, becomes overconfident and begins to talk freely. He thinks he's got the better of the silly, scruffy little detective as Columbo seems to conclude his line of questioning and makes to leave. Almost at the door the detective turns back to the suspect and says, 'Just one more thing.' Colombo points out to the suspect a tiny contradiction in his story that grows and grows as the suspect tries in vain to brush it aside. As the suspect becomes increasingly angry, Columbo proceeds to almost apologetically grind him into the dust exposing his story or alibi as nonsense and proving that he is the guilty party. Columbo is a bit like Socrates in other ways. Small and scruffy. People take him for a fool but eventually he always outsmarts them.

Although Socrates always tried to avoid contradicting himself, was modest enough to admit that he knew nothing for certain and cared only about discovering the truth, his *method* still managed to irritate the hell out of a lot of very powerful people. Eventually they had him executed in 399 BC on trumped up charges of impiety (insulting the gods) and corrupting the youth. This was a particularly shameful act for a city-state that prided itself on its openness and tolerance. Ancient Athens was a democracy, yet it executed its freest thinker and speaker.

Philosophers need to be free to keep on asking awkward questions as this is the only way to get at the truth. This leads us back to a point made earlier about the importance of freedom of thought and expression to the process and activity of philosophy.

Philosophy and free speech

In a brilliant essay he wrote called *On Liberty*, the nineteenth-century English philosopher, John Stuart Mill, argued that freedom or liberty of thought and expression for all people, so long as it does not harm others by provoking on the spot violence, is one of the cornerstones of a truly civilized society. Societies that don't have it for whatever reason are primitive and backward.

Philosophers certainly need freedom of thought and expression, not only to carry out their civilized and civilizing business of questioning everything and searching for the truth, but to develop into philosophers in the first place. Mill argues that to become truly educated and capable of thinking for himself, a person must study a subject from every possible point of view rather than just be indoctrinated into the one point of view people in authority would like him to have. His teachers should constantly challenge all his opinions and sharpen his wits by defying him to defend those opinions. He should be constantly encouraged to subject his beliefs to criticism and appraisal. This is the way in which a mind capable of doing philosophy is formed. As Mill says:

> In the case of any person whose judgment is really deserving of confidence, how has it become so? Because he has kept his mind open to criticism of his opinions and conduct. Because it has been his practice to listen to all that could be said against him; to profit by as much of it as was just, and expound to himself, and on occasion to others, the fallacy of what was fallacious. Because he has felt, that the only way in which a human being can make some approach to knowing the whole of a subject, is by hearing what can

be said about it by persons of every variety of opinion, and studying all modes in which it can be looked at by every character of mind. No wise man ever acquired his wisdom in any mode but this; nor is it in the nature of human intellect to become wise in any other manner. (*On Liberty*, p. 25)

Sadly, it may be the case for some people that by the time they reach adulthood, religious and/or political indoctrination have made their minds so rigid and inflexible and incapable of free, critical thinking that they are incapable of doing philosophy or even understanding what it is. A notable characteristic of such people is that they immediately become offended if you dare, however politely, to question their opinions or disagree with them, as though having an opinion that is different to theirs, let alone voicing it, is the height of ill-manners. This stance of taking offence when challenged is one of the ways in which people with nonsensical opinions prop them up and 'defend' them against philosophical criticism.

Mill also thinks it is more educational for a person to hear opinions expressed by people who actually hold those opinions rather than just hear them second hand from his own teachers. In short, as the old saying goes, there is nothing like getting the message straight from the horse's mouth. So, if a group of students are studying Neo-Nazism, for example, rather than hear about the views of Neo-Nazis from their middle-aged, middle-class, ever so liberal teacher with her designer grey hair, her up-market hippy beads and her passion for folk festivals, they ought to hear about the views of Neo-Nazis from a middle-aged, middle-class, ever so right wing racist, sexist, homophobic Fascist thug with his storm trooper hair cut, his swastika tattoos and his passion for SS uniforms!

This is controversial stuff because there are a lot of well-meaning liberals out there who think that Fascists and racists of all kinds shouldn't be allowed anywhere near educational establishments to attempt to influence the minds of supposedly impressionable young and not so young students. But in Mill's opinion these well-meaning liberals are wrong. These well-meaning liberals want to decide issues for other people who are, or should be, perfectly capable of making up their own minds. Mill says:

> I must be permitted to observe, that it is not the feeling sure of a doctrine (be it what it may) which I call an assumption of infallibility. It is the undertaking to decide that question for others, without allowing them to hear what can be said on the contrary side. And I denounce and reprobate this pretension not the less, if put forth on the side of my most solemn convictions. (*On Liberty*, p. 28)

Also, these well-meaning liberals want to prevent people from hearing all sides of a debate, denying them the only means, according to Mill, of becoming truly wise; the only means of having genuinely *considered* opinions rather than mere *received* opinions. If Neo-Nazi racists are full of shit then the vast majority of students will not only have the intelligence to *tell* they are full of shit but also the confidence to *tell them* they are full of shit. Mill argues that we learn best the value or otherwise of our own opinions by listening to and arguing with those who hold contrary opinions. For this reason a good philosopher will always hear-out the opposition however ridiculous and offensive their viewpoint. Speaking of the person who wants to become truly wise Mill says:

> Nor is it enough, that he should hear the arguments of adversaries from his own teachers, presented as they state them, and accompanied by what they offer as refutations. That is not the way to do justice to the arguments, or bring them into real contact with his own mind. He must be able to hear them from persons who actually believe them; who defend them in earnest, and do their very utmost for them. He must know them in their most plausible and persuasive form; he must feel the whole force of the difficulty which the true view of the subject has to encounter and dispose of; else he will never really possess himself of the portion of truth which meets and removes that difficulty. (*On Liberty*, p. 42)

I once taught *On Liberty* to a very bright, articulate and genuinely liberal-minded philosophy class who wanted to put Mill's views into practice and invite a politically active racist into the lesson in order to 'feel the whole force of the difficulty which the true view of the subject has to encounter and dispose of'. I thought about doing it but in the end chickened out for fear of the controversy it would cause both at the college where I worked and in the popular press who always willfully misunderstand the true context of everything in order to create a scandal and sell newspapers.

There would have been anti-Nazi protestors outside throwing eggs at nationalist skinheads who had rocked-up for a scrap with the anti-Nazi protestors. There would have been thin and not so thin blue lines everywhere, and I would probably have been accused of rubbing shoulders with the British National Party. And anyway, the college, being very politically correct and right-on liberal with its Equal Opportunities Policy, its Equality and Diversity Policy, its Access for All Policy, its every Citizen Matters Policy, its Safeguarding Policy and its Say 'No' To Racism Policy, would not have allowed it.

So, in an ironic, roundabout way, my students were denied their educational and democratic right, denied the opportunity to say a considered and philosophical 'no' to racism, by a well-meaning, misguided, narrow-minded liberalism. Sometimes, ignorant, busybody, politically correct liberals are almost as effective as Fascists at denying people their civil liberties.

The father of western philosophy

So, from what has been said so far, we can see that philosophy is a rational, logical, open-minded, free thinking activity that carefully considers all sides of an argument in an objective and unbiased way in an attempt to search out and establish the truth. Philosophy is also the vast historical accumulation of all the arguments and counter arguments put forward by philosophers over thousands of years as they have undertaken that search. In this sense, philosophy is the history of ideas. As for a philosopher, he or she is simply someone who willingly and even lovingly undertakes the search for the truth for its own sake and is not discouraged by the ridicule and intimidation of the ignorant and corrupt or by fear of what he or she might discover.

Philosophy, as we have seen, seeks the truth largely by exposing contradictions and weaknesses in commonly held views. This is not to say that common sense is always wrong, but it is undoubtedly the case that things are not always as they appear. For example, for thousands of years, common sense, based on appearances, held that the sun goes around the earth. With closer observation and a measure of *reasoning*, however, early astronomers worked out that the earth in fact goes around the sun. Philosophy aims to go beyond mere appearances, beliefs and opinions in the hope of discovering certainty, truth, knowledge, reality.

The effort to go beyond mere appearances and opinions and discover reality and truth is precisely what the philosophy of the ancient Greek philosopher, Plato, is all about. We have already met Socrates. Well, Plato was Socrates' friend and star pupil. Plato was born into a rich and powerful Athenian family in c. 428 BC and was educated from an early age for a career in politics. However, disillusioned by all the political corruption in Athens that eventually led to the unjust execution of Socrates in 399 BC, Plato turned away from politics to focus exclusively on philosophy. Plato took over where Socrates left off and developed Socrates' philosophy into a vast system of ideas about reality, knowledge, human nature, education, society, politics and art.

The big difference between Plato and Socrates was that Socrates never actually wrote anything down. He was strictly a street philosopher, an urban rapper who lived to hang out in market places and on temple steps arguing the back legs off a bucking bronco before persuading it to go for a trot. Plato, on the other hand, wrote about 30 *dialogues*: books written in the form of philosophical conversations between a semi-imaginary Socrates and a succession of hard-pressed interlocutors who each get the full Socrates treatment. Needless to say, Socrates usually 'wins' the arguments, or rather, he is the speaker who gets nearest to the truth, but sometimes the opposition score a valid point before Socrates has them doubling up as a magi-mop.

The most important and famous of Plato's dialogues is *The Republic*. It brilliantly weaves together all the main threads of Plato's philosophy and is widely viewed as possibly the greatest work of philosophy ever written; unsurpassed in its brilliance after nearly two and a half thousand years. *The Republic* and the other dialogues pose just about all the central philosophical questions that still concern western philosophers today. This is not to say that Plato has all the answers, far from it. No philosopher has all the answers and like all philosophers Plato has been much criticized. But he asks all the right questions, questions that set the philosophical ball rolling in highly productive and thought provoking directions. Plato's influence is so huge that he is often referred to as 'The father of western philosophy'. The twentieth-century philosopher, Alfred North Whitehead, even describes the whole of philosophy as 'a series of footnotes to Plato' (*Process and Reality*, p. 39).

The central philosophical questions that Plato posed are these:

1. What is the true nature of reality?
2. How can this reality be known?
3. How should I live given the true nature of reality?

These three questions correspond to the three main branches of philosophy that still exist today in one guise or another. I'll list them for you then look at each one in turn:

1. Metaphysics or ontology.
2. Epistemology or theory of knowledge.
3. Ethics or moral philosophy.

Metaphysics and more Plato

Metaphysics is the branch of philosophy that investigates the fundamental nature and origins of reality, existence, being. 'Why is there something rather than nothing?' is a central metaphysical question. 'Does God exist?' is another. Philosophy and metaphysics were so closely bound together at one time that 'metaphysics' was virtually another word for 'philosophy' and philosophers were often called metaphysicians. 'Meta' means transcending or going beyond, so the very term 'metaphysics' suggests that it is the investigation of whatever is above and beyond the physical. Many modern philosophers – that can mean anyone in the past few hundred years – object to this suggestion as they strongly disagree that there is in fact anything above and beyond the physical; that there are any higher powers or other dimensions above and beyond the everyday world we experience through our senses. Two groups of philosophers who hold anti-metaphysical views and can get quite stroppy in their criticism of all metaphysical thinking are empiricists and existentialists.

Increasingly, the term 'metaphysics' has been replaced by the more neutral term 'ontology', although the basic definition of 'ontology' remains pretty much the same as the basic definition of 'metaphysics' given above. 'Metaphysics' has even become something of a term of abuse; 'metaphysical' becoming a warning label slapped on all religious and quasi-religious theories that attempt to explain this world as an inferior quality by-product secreted by a perfect world existing in a higher, non-physical dimension. The Scottish philosopher, David Hume, a very down to earth empiricist, even said that whenever you come across a book of metaphysics you ought to burn it as 'it can contain nothing but sophistry and illusion' (*Enquiries*, p. 165).

I often find myself agreeing with Hume as he is an excellent philosopher, one of the real heavyweight philosophers and one of the clearest minds I have ever encountered, but I don't agree with him on this particular point. Book burning, with the possible exception of celebrity biographies, is a terrible, totalitarian thing to do. Recall what was said earlier about philosophy and freedom of thought and expression. I suspect Hume said what he said about burning books of metaphysics largely for affect and he would probably have fought tooth and nail to prevent anyone from torching any part of Edinburgh Library. Nonetheless, among the philosophy books Hume judged to be as useful as kindling wood are the complete works of Plato because Plato was a metaphysical thinker to the deepest depths of his metaphysical soul.

Plato thought that the constantly changing, constantly decaying, everyday, material world we see around us doesn't really exist, it is just a mere appearance, a shadow, an illusion cast by a higher reality that can't be sensed but that philosophers can think and reason about. This higher reality is not physical but is comprised of perfect, unchanging, timeless, universal forms or ideas. This is Plato's *Theory of Forms* and it is at the heart of his entire philosophy.

Take the example of circles and circularity. According to Plato, none of the circles in the world are real because none of them are truly circular. Even the most finely engineered round washer made by NASA, for example, will not be perfectly circular in shape, it will expand and contract continually according to the temperature and as soon as it is made it will start to decay. What is real, according to Plato, is the perfect metaphysical form of circularity that exists in the timeless realm of forms. It is only the form of circularity that can be truly known. All the particular, imperfect circles in the world only exist as circles and are recognized as circles because they approximate towards the form of perfect circularity and participate in it. They are mere imperfect shadows of perfect circularity; faint, smudged copies of the flawless original.

The forms are the source of all reality and knowledge and there are forms corresponding to every type of particular thing in the world. There is a perfect form of chairs and a perfect form of humans. The forms are arranged in a hierarchy with the forms of qualities and concepts higher in the pyramid than the forms of physical things. So, the forms of love and justice, for example, are higher than the forms of shoes and pencils. At the top of the pyramid is the form of the Good, the supreme source of everything including the forms. Plato's idea of the Good is a bit like our idea of God, except that the Good is not envisaged as having the personal qualities that God is envisaged as having. As the Good is the supreme being that gives meaning and reality to everything else, that defines everything else, it can't itself be defined. Only a lifetime of philosophical contemplation will give a person a clear understanding or revelation of what the Good is.

In his famous simile of the cave (*The Republic*, 514a), Plato argues that most people are like prisoners trapped in a cave looking at shadows on a wall. Knowing no better, the prisoners mistake the shadows for reality and their beliefs about the shadows for knowledge. Only education in abstract subjects like mathematics, followed by the study of philosophy, allows people to escape the cave of ignorance into the clear light of reason and truth. Some people are blinded by the light outside the cave, it overwhelms and terrifies them and they want nothing more than to crawl back into the darkness and place their faith in the unreal shadows once more; in soap operas and fashion magazines and the stuff and nonsense of excessive material wealth. Others become accustomed to the light. They learn to love reason and truth above all else and for their own sake. They come to despise the shadows they once mistook for reality, though they pity the ignorant and weak minded who are still fooled by the shadows and undertake to help them.

Interestingly, Plato thought that only philosophers should become leaders, what he called philosopher kings, because only philosophers are able to distinguish between true reality and mere appearance, between what is so and what only appears to be so. Only philosophers will govern according to reason. Anyone else, anyone still inside the cave, will govern according to their desires, abusing their position for personal advantage. To see that Plato has a point we only have to look at the way many of our politicians behave, fiddling their expenses and involving themselves in corruption and scandal. Philosophers don't desire to govern, they would rather sit in peace on top of a mountain meditating on the perfect, eternal forms, but they govern out of fear of someone less able doing the job. Plato very wisely argued that any-one who desires political power shouldn't be allowed to have it.

Epistemology and more Plato

Epistemology has nothing to do with research into diseases affecting the urinary tract. It is a much drier affair than that. Derived from the Greek word for knowledge: *epistēmē*, *epistemology* is the technical name for theory of knowledge. Theory of knowledge is the branch of philosophy that investigates the nature and possibility of knowledge. Some of the main questions in epistemology are: 'What is know-ledge?', 'What is it to know something?', 'What are the limits of knowledge?' and 'Is knowledge possible?' These questions are all very closely related, especially the first two, because if you can say what it is to know something then you have pretty much said what know-ledge is. Some philosophers, including Plato, have attempted to define what knowledge is by setting rigorous standards for knowing when we have it. Not surprisingly, philosophers disagree endlessly about these standards, accusing each other of not *knowing* that their stand-ard for knowing is as certain and reliable as they believe it is. The slightly weird thing about theory of knowledge is that it very quickly gets applied to itself because as soon as a philosopher claims to know what knowledge is, another philosopher will ask, 'How do you know that you know?'

Plato defined knowledge as justified, true belief. This has come to be known as the JTB analysis of knowledge. It remains the classic def-inition of what knowledge is and although it has been much criticized over the centuries it has stood the test of time pretty well. According to Plato, we only have knowledge if and when the following 3 conditions are satisfied:

1. *The Truth Condition.* What a person knows must be true otherwise he can't be said to know it. This is not to say that knowing something makes it true, simply that something can't be known unless it is true. For example, I can't know that Paris is the capital of England because it is not true that Paris is the capital of England.
2. *The Belief Condition.* A person can't be said to know something unless he also believes it. It would be nonsense to say, 'I know my house is on fire but I don't believe it.' Admittedly, like Victor Meldrew in the British sitcom, *One Foot in the Grave,* many people are in the habit of exclaiming 'I don't believe it!' every time something goes wrong, but this is merely an ironic turn of phrase expressing the wish that an all too real present disaster wasn't happening or the emotional difficulty of coming to terms with it. So, I *can* believe what I don't know, but I *can't* know what I don't believe.
3. *The Justification Condition.* In order for a person to be said to know something his claim to knowledge must be justified. That is, there must be sufficient *evidence* in the case of claims about the physical, empirical world he encounters through his senses, or sufficient *proof* in the case of logical and mathematical claims based on pure reason and deduction.

The justification condition remains the most controversial of Plato's three conditions. Wrangling over it keeps many a philosopher in a cushy university job. The debate focuses on what constitutes sufficient evidence on the empirical side of things and sufficient proof on the logical, purely rational side of things. Some philosophers called *rationalists* – Plato was a rationalist – argue that empirical evidence is just too unreliable ever to give us knowledge. This is mainly because the senses, the sense organs, can't ever be trusted to give us totally reliable information about the world. We are too easily fooled by optical illusions, ambiguous images, tricks of the light, hallucinations, our desire for things to be the way we want them to be and so on. If knowledge is possible, it is only pure reason, pure thought, that can produce it. So, according to a rationalist, I can *know* that 1+1=2 because this is a matter of pure reason and logic, 1+1 *means* 2. However, I can't *know* that the sky is blue because all claims that the sky is blue depend on unreliable senses, mine and other people's. I can only ever *believe* that the sky is blue, but belief by itself is not knowledge. According to rationalists, the only true knowledge is what they call *a priori* knowledge. That is, purely rational knowledge gained prior to or apart from sensory experience.

Some philosophers called *global sceptics* insist that it is impossible to know anything at all for certain, empirically or rationally, but of course we can immediately begin to play the epistemological game with them and ask them how they *know* this. Other philosophers called *academic sceptics* try to doubt everything with the ultimately positive aim of finding something that can't be doubted, something absolutely certain and indubitable. We will take a closer look at academic scepticism in the next chapter.

There isn't scope in this introduction to look at and evaluate all the different standards for knowing that philosophers have proposed and rejected over the centuries. The whole business of epistemology can, as you have probably already guessed, get rather complex. It includes much of the history of philosophy. If you want to know more, there are hundreds if not thousands of books that deal with the subject of epistemology in meticulous, epistemological detail. Try *An Introduction to the Theory of Knowledge* by Dan O'Brien, or the classic, *The Problem of Knowledge* by A. J. Ayer. That ought to keep you busy for a while.

The philosophy of doing the right thing

The branch of philosophy that investigates the moral value of human activity and the rules and principles that ought to govern it is called ethics or moral philosophy. All the great philosophers, it seems fair to say, are ultimately interested in ethics. Answering ethical questions is the ultimate goal of all their philosophizing. This is certainly true of Socrates, Plato, Aristotle, Aquinas, Hume, Kant, Nietzsche, Rousseau, Kierkegaard, Wittgenstein, Sartre and de Beauvoir, to name but a few. They seek to answer metaphysical and epistemological questions about what there is and how we know it in order to answer moral questions about how we should live given what we know about what there is. A philosopher who decides, for example, that he knows God exists is likely to draw very different conclusions about the value and purpose of human life and how it ought and ought not to be lived than a philosopher who decides he knows God doesn't exist.

By the way, ethical questions are philosophical questions because questions about moral values can't really be answered by science or any other practical discipline. For example, science can deal with a practical question like, 'Is John a natural blond?', but it can't really deal with a moral question like, 'Is John good?' A scientist could investigate what John does and maybe even look into why he does it, but a philosopher would still be needed to explain *why* John's behaviour is or is not morally good – although there are some philosophers who think that such an explanation is impossible because all moral statements are meaningless! We will come to them shortly.

Some moral philosophers called *deontologists* argue that certain human actions are wrong in themselves; that there are fixed moral truths or principles that apply to every person regardless of their circumstances. They think that these unchanging moral truths or principles can be discovered or established through pure reason; that ethics too is a matter of *a priori* knowledge. Other moral philosophers called *consequentialists* argue that no human action is right or wrong in itself. The rightness or wrongness of an action has to be judged according to the consequences it produces.

The best-known consequentialists, the *utilitarians*, argue that if an action contributes to the sum total of human happiness it is a morally good action, if it contributes to the sum total of human suffering it is a morally bad action. Utilitarians disagree with deontologists that ethics is a matter of *a priori* knowledge or reasoning. For them, ethics is a common sense business involving the practical, empirical assessment of the consequences of human actions in the real world. The split between deontologists and utilitarians, with the former looking to pure reason to decide questions of right and wrong and the latter looking to empirical evidence, is yet another aspect of the great divide in philosophy between rationalists and empiricists; between rationalism and empiricism.

Although they are either side of one of philosophy's greatest divides, both deontologists and utilitarians are, broadly speaking, moral objectivists. That is, they believe that there are objective moral facts, or at least, that there are objective means of establishing that an action is right or wrong. They simply disagree about the means. This sets them apart from various groups of philosophers who are very sceptical that there is any genuine way of *judging* right from wrong. These philosophers, collectively known as moral subjectivists, argue that there are no moral truths or principles, that ethical statements are neither true nor false but are essentially meaningless. They argue that what appear to be moral assertions laying claim to underlying moral principles, such as 'Giving to charity is good' or 'Stealing is wrong', are really just expressions of feeling and emotion, expressions of approval or disapproval. The philosopher A. J. Ayer stated the subjectivist position without pulling any punches when he wrote:

> If now I generalise my previous statement and say, 'Stealing money is wrong,' I produce a sentence which has no factual meaning – that is, express no proposition which can be either true or false. It is as if I had written 'stealing money!!' – where the shape and thickness of the exclamation marks show, by a suitable convention, that a special sort of moral disapproval is the feeling which is being expressed. It is clear that there is nothing said here which can be true or false. (*Language, Truth and Logic*, p. 110)

One of the best-known groups of subjectivists are called *emotivists*. They argue, for example, that although the disagreement between people on either side of the animal rights issue is very real in terms of the animosity each side feels for the views and actions of the other, there is no solving the disagreement by moral argument because there are no moral facts of the matter to be discovered or worked out that would ever allow a person to conclude that one side is wrong and the other side right! Those who want to protect animals simply feel one way, those who want to experiment on them or hunt them for fun simply feel another way. According to emotivists, saying, 'Hunting animals for fun is wrong', is just a fancy way of exclaiming, 'Hunting animals – boo!', while saying, 'Experimenting on animals is good', is just a fancy way of exclaiming, 'Experimenting on animals – hurray!' Not surprisingly, emotivism has been given the silly but rather appropriate nickname of the 'boo-hurray' theory of ethics.

Some narrow-minded, reactionary types have claimed that it is immoral to claim that morality has no basis in fact because to do so licenses people to do as they please. Claiming that morality has no basis in fact may well encourage some people to do as they please, but it is nonetheless very poor philosophizing indeed to insist that philosophers have a moral obligation to argue that morality has a basis in fact even if reason suggests that it doesn't. As Hume so brilliantly puts it:

> There is no method of reasoning more common, and yet none more blame-able, than, in philosophical disputes, to endeavour the refutation of any hypo-thesis, by a pretence of its dangerous consequences to religion and morality. When any opinion leads to absurdities, it is certainly false, but it is not certain that an opinion is false because it is of dangerous consequence. Such topics, therefore, ought entirely to be forborne; as serving nothing to the discovery of truth, but only to make the person of an antagonist odious. (*Enquiries*, p. 96)

Interestingly, an emotivist will argue that anyone who appeals to moral-ity in a desperate attempt to defend the objectivity of morality is merely expressing a feeling of disapproval; booing emotivism and giving it the thumbs down. In the end, the only serious way to challenge moral subjectivism is to successfully make a reasonable, non-moralizing case for some form of moral objectivism.

In outlining what ethics is it is useful to identify its 3 main branches, which are: (1) normative ethics or moral theory, (2) meta-ethics and (3) practical or applied ethics.

1. *Normative Ethics or Moral Theory*: Normative ethics attempts to for-
   mulate general principles for distinguishing good from bad, right
   from wrong. It attempts to find a coherent and defensible basis for
   ethical principles and values. There are basically 3 normative moral
   theories: (a) deontological or duty based ethics, (b) utilitarianism
   and (c) virtue theory. I've already briefly mentioned the first two,
   but it is useful to say a bit more. Sorry to further divide my sub-
   divisions – I honestly try to avoid such irritating, anorakish practices
   in my writing – but here is a brief outline of each one in turn:
   (a) *Deontological or duty based ethics*: This, as we've seen, holds
       that there are fixed, universally applicable moral principles that
       can be worked out by reason. The most famous deontologist is
       the German philosopher, Immanuel Kant. When philosophy stu-
       dents study this moral theory they invariably study Kant's ideas
       on ethics. In fact, the terms 'Kantian ethics' and 'deontological
       ethics' have become virtually synonymous.

       At the heart of Kant's moral theory is a principle know as the
       categorical imperative. It appears at first to involve doing to oth-
       ers as you would have them do to you, but more precisely it
       involves asking yourself, 'What if everyone did this?', before you
       go ahead and do whatever it is you're thinking of doing. If it is
       the sort of thing that would become impossible for anyone to
       do if everyone tried to do it all the time then it is your moral duty
       not to do it.

       Take lying, for example. Lying only works if the person you are
       lying to believes you are telling the truth. Lying is a parasite on

the convention of truth telling. If everyone tried to tell lies all the time then there could be no convention of truth telling because nobody would ever believe anything that anyone said. In such a situation it would be impossible to lie, that is, to tell a lie that succeeded. Kant argues that you should only act on maxims that you can will to become a universal law. The maxim that it is ok to lie that I establish every time I lie can't be willed as a universal law in the way that truth telling, for example, can be willed as a universal law. It is possible for everyone to tell the truth universally, but it is not possible for everyone to lie universally.

There is another strand to Kant's moral theory that goes like this: If I lie to someone, or break a promise to them, or steal from them, or rape them, or murder them, then I'm using them for my own ends and goals rather than respecting them as a free being with their own ends and goals. In Kant's terms, I'm treating them as a mere means rather than as an end in themselves. Of course, we all treat each other as a means. I use the taxi driver as a means to getting to the station and he uses me as a means to earn a living, but this arrangement is or should be consensual, both parties have entered into it freely. I have used the taxi driver as a means but not as a *mere* means. I have not disrespected his freedom and right to self-determination as I would do if I refused to pay him or mugged him at the end of the journey.

Kant envisaged a *kingdom of ends*, a world in which people never use each other as a mere means and always respect each other as free, rational ends in themselves. This, for Kant, would be the ideal moral state. A distant dream perhaps, but something worth aiming for.

(b) *Utilitarianism*: This, as we've seen, holds that no human action is right or wrong in itself. The moral value of an action has to be judged according to the *utility*, the usefulness, of its consequences. For utilitarians the only real measure of moral goodness is what tends to make reasonably well-adjusted people happy: the absence of pain, physical and mental pleasure, decent food, sanitation, shelter, respect from others, friends, something constructive to do and so on. Utilitarians argue, quite sensibly, that to discover what makes people happy you only have to look at what it is most people the world over want and have always wanted. Nobody wants to be in constant pain, live in squalor and be abused by others; if they do, there is something warped about them. We could say that such warped people no longer know what they want.

The most famous utilitarians are Jeremy Bentham, James Mill and his son John Stuart Mill, a philosopher we've already met. Bentham is a less sophisticated utilitarian than John Stuart Mill and tends to equate happiness with bodily pleasure. He is criticized for placing all pleasures on the same scale, for lumping the trivial game of push pin in with poetry. John Stuart Mill, being a more subtle thinker, says that pleasures are not just quantitatively different but qualitatively different as well. There is a need to distinguish between higher and lower pleasures. Mill argues that those who have genuinely experienced both higher and lower pleasures know that higher pleasures are more valuable and rewarding than lower pleasures. So, there is a far greater quality of pleasure to be had from listening to Mozart than from eating an ice cream, although of course you could listen to Mozart while eating an ice cream.

Utilitarianism is perhaps easier to grasp than Kantian ethics because it is a more down to earth, practical theory. However, it can lack precision. Whereas Kant is very clear about what you shouldn't do, Mill and company have to play the game of assessing the consequences of actions and types of action to see if they add to or detract from the sum total of human happiness. Sometimes it is easy to see that an action, a rape, for example, has caused a vast amount of suffering and misery and only provided a sick temporary pleasure to the scumbag who did it. But often it is not so easy to decide if an action has, on balance, produced more happiness than unhappiness. Buying expensive drugs to help a cancer patient obviously produces happiness for the patient and his family but what if the same money could have been spent saving the lives of 20 babies who died? Whatever the strengths and weaknesses of utilitarianism as a moral theory, in a world of limited resources people are constantly forced to make difficult utilitarian decisions whether they like it or not.

(c) *Virtue Theory*: We've not come across this moral theory before. It is the most ancient of the three moral theories we are considering, dating back to the time of the ancient Greeks and, once again, that man Aristotle. Aristotle wrote a book called the *Nicomachean Ethics*, named after his son, Nicomachus, who edited it. It's amazing that Aristotle found time to have children as well as do all that philosophizing, but that is precisely what his ethics is all about: living life to the max by building a well rounded, balanced life in which you don't deprive yourself in one area of your existence by overdoing it in another.

Aristotle was a teleologist, which means he thought that everything in nature has its own *telos*, the true and proper end goal at which it aims. The *telos* of an acorn, for example, is to become a healthy oak tree that produces healthy acorns of its own. For a thing to achieve its *telos* is for it to flourish. Aristotle's virtue theory seeks to identify the personal virtues that facilitate human flourishing, the virtues that enable a person to forge a full, worthwhile, successful, satisfying life, the virtues that lead to the state of profound happiness and contentment that the ancient Greeks called *eudaimonia*. The virtues that facilitate human flourishing accord with what Aristotle calls the *golden mean* ('mean' as in 'middle').

The Aristotelian notion of the golden mean is remarkably similar to Gautama Buddha's notion of the middle way. Great minds think alike, even if they love to disagree over details. To strike the golden mean or the middle way, a person must achieve a balance, a happy medium, between various vices of deficiency and excess in the way he approaches his life and other people. The Buddha once said something like, 'A person is like a musical instrument. His life is the tune he plays. If he is too slack or too uptight in the way he lives then his life will be out of tune.'

The virtue of generosity, for example, lies between the deficiency of meanness and the excess of profligacy. A person who is mean and stingy will be disliked, will receive few favours from others and will fail to resource his everyday existence adequately. A person who is profligate and throws his money around, on the other hand, will be exploited by others and will diminish his assets to the extent that he can no longer support himself and his dependents. A person who strikes the golden mean of generosity will be genuinely liked and respected, will find pleasure in pleasing people, will keep enough in reserve to prevent himself and his dependents from becoming a burden on others and will be able to legitimately and successfully call in favours should he ever need any.

Now, importantly, what constitutes generosity, or any other virtue, will depend on a person's particular circumstances. Obviously, what is generosity for a rich man will be profligacy for a poor man and so on. The ancient Greeks inscribed the aphorisms 'Know thyself' and 'Nothing to excess' on the temple of Apollo at Delphi, thought to be the centre of the world, and it was widely understood in their culture that every person must try to use their worldly wisdom and their self-knowledge to work out what is the happy medium for them. Some people can tolerate more alcohol than others, some people have a stronger nerve in tense or dangerous situations than others, some people have a naturally healthy constitution while others don't. We have all been dealt different hands in life, by chance or by the gods, it's how we play the hand we've been dealt that matters.

Aristotle's moral theory is not a rulebook, dogmatically saying you must do this, you must not do that. It is a general philosophical and practical guide to living that invites each individual to honestly and intelligently assess his unique character and situation in order to decide the details of how he should conduct himself in order to achieve happiness.

2. *Meta-Ethics*: While metaphysics investigates the fundamental nature and origins of existence, meta-ethics investigates the fundamental nature of ethics; the nature and status of moral thought and discourse. It does not get involved in actual moral disagreements, it explores instead the nature of moral disagreement as such and ponders why it exists. It is distinct from normative ethics in that it is not concerned with establishing principles for distinguishing right from wrong. It is concerned instead with what 'right' and 'wrong' and other moral terms like them actually mean, if indeed they mean anything at all. For example, a key question in meta-ethics has and always will be, 'What is the meaning of "good"?' That is, what does it mean to say a person or action is morally good as opposed to saying a person or action is good for some purpose or other? A man who is good at murdering is a good murderer but that is not to say he is a good man.

Meta-ethics also considers the possibility that it may not really mean anything to say, for example, 'Honesty is good.' That is, meta-ethics considers the possibility that there are no moral facts or truths. We came across this issue earlier when looking at the debate between moral objectivists and moral subjectivists. We can now see that the objectivist/subjectivist debate is a central feature of meta-ethics. Whatever side meta-ethicists take in the debate, they are all interested in the contrast between facts and values and the differences between ordinary statements and moral statements.

They get particularly excited about what they call 'ought statements' such as, 'You ought to respect your elders.' The fascinating thing about ought statements, the reason why meta-ethicists get so steamed up about them, is that they don't just describe situations – 'The grass is green, the sky is blue' – they prescribe, recommend, even urge certain behaviours. Ought statements don't just tell you something, they tell you that you have a moral obligation to do or not do something. But do ought statements really mean anything? They seem to appeal to some fact of the matter, to claim, for example, that it is *true* that you ought to respect your elders, but perhaps ought statements are really just expressions of a person's desire for you to behave in a certain manner, to respect your elders or whatever. A polite way of saying, 'I want you to respect your elders' or even, 'Respect your elders or else!' A polite way that is more likely to get you to behave in a certain manner than if they just bluntly ordered you to do it. The debate continues.

3. *Practical or Applied Ethics*: This is the branch of ethics most people are familiar with. Audience participation chat shows on TV and radio love to raise a wrangle over the most contentious practical ethical issues of the day, usually without much coherence or direction – drugs, abortion, animal rights, what to do with teenagers, euthanasia, child labour, prostitution, carbon emissions, pornography, whatever. The aim, of course, is to provoke maximum controversy and disagreement for the sake of boosting ratings and advertising revenues, rather than actually resolve anything. Some idiot chips in with their precious pennyworth of opinion. Everyone who already agrees with that person claps and cheers, and those who don't tut-tut, grimace, boo or even become abusive. Nobody changes their mind about anything, that would be a humiliating defeat, and everyone leaves with the same half-baked prejudices with which they arrived.

Philosophers try to do a bit better than this. It is the same practical ethical issues as the mob that they are interested in, but they try to look at them objectively and dispassionately, with an open mind, without feeling that they have to take one side or the other, at least until they reach the end of balanced deliberations that have given a fair hearing to both sides. As we saw earlier, it is in the very nature of philosophy to weigh all sides of an argument. Most importantly, philosophers apply the various normative ethical theories to whatever practical ethical issues they are focused on to see what emerges. They will ask and seek to answer questions like, 'What is the utilitarian position on drug taking?' or 'What conclusions does Kantian ethics help us draw about the rights and wrongs of euthanasia?'

Practical ethics can be studied for its own sake, but it also has clear applications in the real world. Medical ethics, for example, is an area of practical ethics that applies the findings of normative ethics to real life and death situations using the full range of philosophical methods. Hospitals, for example, employ philosophically trained experts in medical ethics to advise doctors, patients and the relatives of patients on such ethically sensitive matters as organ donation, continuation and withdrawal of life support, abortion, the rights of the mentally ill, the separation or non-separation of conjoined twins and so on and so forth.

There is a lot more to ethics than I have had the opportunity to tell you about here. In summarizing utilitarianism, for example, I was acutely aware of all the things I was leaving out of my account that John Stuart Mill includes in his in order to forestall various criticisms and reservations. But then, this is not a book about ethics but a guide on how to become a philosopher that includes a very general introduction to what philosophy is. It is enough for you to know that ethics is a very important part of philosophy and what ethics involves in a general sense.

If you'd like to get further under the skin of ethics and explore what, if anything, it all means, if normative, meta and practical ethics turn you on or float your boat, then I place you in the capable hands of the authors of the many hundreds of specialist books that have been written on the vast topic of ethics. Try *Ethics: Inventing Right and Wrong* by J. L. Mackie or *Being Good: A Short Introduction to Ethics* by Simon

Blackburn. These works should keep you busy for a while, especially if you are super keen and have also decided to read those books I recommended earlier on epistemology.

Summary

Recall the first of the dictionary definitions of the term 'philosophy' given earlier: 'Philosophy is the rational investigation of being, knowledge and right conduct.' Note how this definition fits perfectly with the three main branches of philosophy I've outlined. The rational investigation of being is metaphysics or ontology, the rational investigation of knowledge is epistemology or theory of knowledge and the rational investigation of right conduct is ethics or moral philosophy. The dictionary always gets it spot on and you can learn a lot about philosophy just by looking up the meaning of philosophy-related words in a dictionary.

If you are really serious about becoming a philosopher you might even want to get hold of a dictionary of philosophy – a very useful A–Z guide to famous philosophers, schools of philosophy and philosophical terms. There are lots of different philosophy dictionaries on the market to choose from, published by Pan, Penguin, Oxford, Cambridge, Collins and Routledge. I wouldn't like to appear as though I was rubbing shoulders with a particular publisher by recommending one over another, so take your pick. Just be careful you don't confuse food for thought with thought of food and mistakenly buy the *Kitchenary Dictionary and Philosophy of Italian Cooking*.

So, you now know something about philosophy as an activity and a subject, as much as my whirlwind tour could provide in the space available, enough to get you started. You have learnt some key philosophical terms and the names and ideas of some major philosophers. In so far as you have reflected on, questioned and criticized these ideas in your own mind as you have read through this chapter, you have started philosophizing and are therefore already a philosopher – although you were probably already a philosopher before you picked up this book, even if you didn't realize it.

Hopefully, reading Chapter 1 and thinking about all the ideas in it has whetted your appetite for doing more philosophy; for really getting your head stuck into some classic, juicy philosophical problems to see how they taste. I'm confident you are more than ready to polish off the next chapter. Take it steady though. That way you'll get the full flavour of the problems and issues while avoiding the mental indigestion that can cause a sudden loss of appetite in new diners at philosophy's rich, dry feast.

2 How to be a Philosopher – Phase One: Doubting Everything

As I said in the Introduction, anyone who has ever thought philosophically, which is just about everyone, is already a philosopher. I ran into a friend the other day in town while buying socks in M&S. I don't know how we got onto the subject so quickly amongst all that 100% cotton but she told me she knew three people with cancer who were not very old. She said it made her think about life and death and what it is all about. We discussed the importance of making the most of life while you still can and how some people fail to do so. If this wasn't a philosophical conversation I don't know what is. Admittedly, we each had our own shopping to do, places to go and people to see, so the conversation didn't last long enough to penetrate the thoughts of the great philosophers on the subject of making the most of life while you still can, but it was at least an informal philosophical conversation that could have gone further and deeper, become more structured and formal, had there been more time and fewer distractions.

Philosophy pops up everywhere and the vast majority of people are philosophers pretty often. The strangeness of life, the inevitability of suffering and death, the peculiar fact that most people seem to remain quite cheerful and positive despite what they endure on a daily basis, are all grounds for philosophical reflection. 'It makes you think, doesn't it,' people muse, having just watched a TV documentary about the

vastness of outer space or having just sent grandma on her final journey at the local crematorium.

So, we are all philosophers broadly speaking, in a vague, dreamy
sort of a way. On one level, that creates a problem for me in writing
this book as it seems to defeat my object. As I said way back, the big
irony for me is that I'm writing this book to tell people how to become
something they almost certainly are already! But then again, I don't
want to show you how to philosophize in a vague, almost dreamy sort
of a way. That can't be taught anyway. No. I want to show you how to
philosophize in a lucid and alert way. In a more structured, rational,
productive and formal way than perhaps you have up to now. Dare I
say it, I want to help you to philosophize properly; to philosophize with
a degree of coherence and direction rather than just muse nebulously
about how mysterious life is and how insignificant we all are in the
grand scheme of things.

Philosophizing properly

As with most things, to become a proper philosopher you need to
learn to walk before you can run. Rather than shoot the breeze in a
directionless, rambling way about the very biggest, broadest philosophical problems, you actually need to begin by considering smaller,
more specific, more immediate philosophical problems concerning
what is, or appears to be, directly in front of your eyes. You need to
begin by questioning and doubting what is supposed to be glaringly
obvious and beyond dispute about the everyday world around you.
Eventually, your knowledge of these smaller, more specific, more
immediate philosophical problems, not to mention the thinking tech-
niques you will acquire simply by thinking about them, will give you the
confidence and informed philosophical vision to have a serious stab at
the bigger questions, or at least to see what the bigger questions are
really asking.

For example, rather than get nowhere trying to dream up a definitive answer to the very vague philosophical question, 'What is the meaning of life?', you will be able to think constructively about what this question actually means; what, if anything, it is actually asking and the strengths and weaknesses of the various answers that can and have been given to it. Perhaps none of this will satisfy you as an answer to the question, 'What is the meaning of life?', but then unlike religion, philosophy doesn't claim to have all or even any of the answers. It simply tries to understand certain questions and problems accurately and to offer a few possible answers. It limits itself to doing this because if there is one thing philosophers have learnt down through the millennia of philosophizing it is that if you try to go further than logic and reason will allow you to go, you immediately start making assumptions and jumping to conclusions. In short, you start guessing, which is fantasizing not philosophizing.

So, in a moment I'm going to ask you to start philosophizing properly in a structured, rational, productive, formal way by considering a smallish, specific and immediate philosophical problem concerning the world you are in, or that you believe you are in, right now. I'm going to ask you to question and doubt what is supposed to be glaringly obvious and beyond dispute. I'm going to ask you to be a philosophical sceptic.

According to the dictionary, a *sceptic* is 'a person who habitually doubts the authenticity of accepted beliefs'. Scepticism is right at the heart of every philosophical project and all philosophers are sceptics to some extent. Philosophers are not prepared to accept anything at face value, so they sceptically ask questions and raise doubts about beliefs that other people take entirely for granted. Most philosophers, you may be pleased to hear, do not indulge in all this negativity just for the sake of it. Most are actually searching for a positive outcome. They are, as I mentioned earlier, *academic sceptics*, philosophers who try, as an academic exercise, to doubt everything with the ultimate aim of finding something that can't be doubted; something absolutely certain and indubitable. It is relatively easy for you to play this game too. Anyone can be an academic sceptic; they just have to be prepared to think outside the box.

Obviously, I don't know where you are reading this book. You might be at your kitchen table, standing on a train, lying in a park or sitting on a boulder halfway up a mountain. What I'm a little more certain about is that wherever you are you are surrounded by objects, or, at least, that it seems to you that you are surrounded by objects. This book is one of them. You can see, hear, touch, smell or taste the many objects around you. Of course, you may not have all your senses intact. You may be blind or deaf or both, but I trust you have enough of your senses intact to be aware you are surrounded by objects, otherwise you would not be able to read this book in print or Braille or have it read to you.

The point I'm making is that your senses constantly inform you in no uncertain terms that what philosophers call *the external world* is out there, surrounding you, right now. It insists on being there and doing its own thing regardless of what you do. You can ignore parts of it, but only by focusing on other parts and you can't make it vanish altogether. Even your own body is a part of it. A special kind of object for sure, but an object or collection of objects nonetheless. In short, nothing seems more sure, certain, irrefutable, indubitable and unquestionable than that the external world is out there. Only a madman would try to deny it. A madman or a philosopher – a philosopher being a kind of madman in the opinion of the mob.

So, without wishing you to feel you are losing your mind, or to think that I'm losing mine, that is precisely what I want you to do now. I want you to try to deny it. I want you to try and think of any and every reason you can, however crazy it sounds, for doubting the existence of the external world. To make your philosophical task easier, take a particular object and focus on that. This book, a cup, a rock, a blade of grass, the building opposite – it doesn't matter. Rather boringly, I'm at home in my study as usual so I will take this rather nice black gel pen and doubt its existence in every way I can.

I get my philosophy students to do this exercise, to play the doubt-ing game. We all sit around doubting in every way possible the exist-ence of the plastic water bottle I always have with me. I used to get them to doubt the existence of a heavy brass candlestick, with a candle burning in it and everything, but then I wondered why I was bothering to take a heavy, cumbersome brass candlestick to college when any object will do just as well. Lighting the candle was also against the col-lege health and safety policy.

Sometimes to do philosophy properly you need to get right away from books and just think. You need to forget about everything else and get intimate with your own grey matter. As Nietzsche writes, 'To become a thinker. – How can anyone become a thinker if he does not spend at least a third of the day without passions, people and books?' (The Wan-derer and his Shadow, 324, p. 390). What Nietzsche neglects to mention here, although he knew it well, is that it is often useful while thinking to make a few notes. 'Writing is thinking' my old professor used to say. So, I'll stop banging on and quoting Nietzsche and you put this book down and I'll meet you at the start of the next paragraph in 20 minutes or so when you have listed as many reasons as you can think of for doubting the existence of whatever object it is you have chosen to doubt . . . .

Now, how was that for you? Did it hurt to do some philosophy rather than just read about it or was it a pleasure to get your neurons buzzing?

Over the years, my beloved philosophy students have come up with all sorts of weird and wonderful reasons for doubting the existence of the water bottle, the candlestick or whatever. Here are some of them. How do their reasons compare with yours?

Hallucination and optical illusion

One of the reasons my philosophy students most commonly give for doubting the existence of what appears to be there before them is hallucination. An hallucination is the false perception of an object when no object is present. The term 'hallucination' refers to the experience of hallucinating rather than to what is hallucinated. A person doesn't *see* hallucinations because the whole point of hallucination is that there is nothing there. A person *has* hallucinations, or to be more precise, he hallucinates. A person hallucinates because his mind is disordered in some way. What he fancies he sees (or hears) is a subjective projection into the world. It is not the world playing tricks on him, but his own mind playing tricks on him. It is possible to hallucinate anything. A water bottle or a candlestick or far more weird and wonderful objects. If the stories we hear are to be believed, people tend to hallucinate scary things like spiders and scorpions, or bizarre things like leprechauns. It seems that the mental disorder that causes people to hallucinate dredges images up from the darkest depths of their subconscious.

In *Fear and Loathing in Las Vegas: A Savage Journey to the Heart of the American Dream*, a novel by Hunter S. Thompson, the central character, Duke, hallucinates his dead grandmother crawling up his leg with a knife in her teeth – bizarre and scary! 'Hallucinations are bad enough,' says Duke. 'But after a while you learn to cope with things like seeing your dead grandmother crawling up your leg with a knife in her teeth. Most acid fanciers can handle this sort of thing' (*Fear and Loathing in Las Vegas*, p. 47). Duke is high on an unfeasibly strong cocktail of hallucinogenic drugs, including LSD and mescaline, and it is drug-fuelled hallucinations that we most commonly hear about thanks to the excesses of rock stars and radical writers.

In *Lucy in the Sky with Diamonds* (LSD), for example, The Beatles sing about a girl with kaleidoscope eyes and taxis made of newspaper appearing on the shore that wait to take you away. Bizarrely, band member and writer of the song, John Lennon, always insisted on denying that it is about drugs, but to anyone who has done fewer drugs than Lennon did it is obvious that it is about drugs, as band member and co-writer of the song, Paul McCartney, confirmed in 1994.

For his part, the French existentialist philosopher, Jean-Paul Sartre, had himself injected with mescaline under experimental conditions in 1935. He wanted to have a genuine hallucinatory experience so he could analyse it in a book he was writing on the imagination. As he tells us in that book, *The Imaginary*, he managed to hallucinate three small parallel clouds that appeared to float before him in the hospital room where he was sitting (*The Imaginary*, p. 156). All rather mundane compared to kaleidoscope eyes, psychedelic newspaper taxis or night-marish dagger-biting old ladies, but it was sufficient material, or should I say non-material, for him to analyse. He got the results he wanted even if the rest of the experience was a thoroughly bad trip that haunted him for years.

So, it is possible, however unlikely, that any object that appears to be before you now, isn't really there. It is possible that that pencil or that cup or that King Kong key ring or that taxi do not exist, that they are merely projections of a mind deranged by drugs, alcohol, fever, mental disorder, hypnosis or all of them together!

We can sometimes be led to think things are there when they are not, not by hallucinations but by various tricks of the light and so on. If I see a mirage of a lake in the distance, for example, this is not an hal-lucination. I'm not being tricked by my mind into thinking something is there that isn't, but by certain external, objective conditions of light and heat. As most people know from their travels or from watching all those desert movies and documentaries, the apparent lake is just heat haze; hot and dusty air shimmering away to the horizon.

It is possible that anything I believe to be real and present is just an optical illusion produced by a trick of the light, a magician's smoke and mirrors or some kind of holographic projection. It is unlikely, perhaps, that the phone on my desk is really just an optical illusion. After all, it looks so solid, so sure of itself, and I seem to recall having used it earlier. But it is nonetheless possible and certainly not beyond the bounds of philosoph-ical doubt that it is an optical illusion. It is possible to doubt its existence on these seemingly crazy grounds, at least for philosophical purposes.

All this talk of hallucinating and optical illusions tends to focus on this or that particular thing not being real. I asked you to focus on doubting the reality of this or that particular thing, rather than everything, in order to make the exercise a little more straightforward. But what if everything that appears to be around you now is not really there at all?

Appearance and reality

What if you are in fact a bodiless brain in a vat of special nutrients sitting on a shelf in a basement laboratory on a planet in a far away galaxy? Actually, I don't know why it has to be a far away galaxy, you could be a brain in a vat in a local laboratory just a mile away from where you think you are now. The special nutrients keep the brain that you are alive and a group of mad scientists working on some dastardly government project pump your apparent awareness of the world into you through a series of electrodes plugged in all over your outer cortex.

It's a very complex business making you perceive that you are sitting in a library reading this book, or lounging by a flower bed in the park on a hot summer day, when you are really just a pickled organ, so the scientists have a super-computer to take care of all the input. It's certainly an excellent programme that puts PS3 and X-Box to shame. In fact, they are only a tiny part of its programme. It not only takes care of what you believe you are seeing, but also what you believe you are hearing, smelling, tasting and touching. It manages to convince you that you have a body that is capable of intricate movements; a body that feels hot and cold, hunger and thirst, pleasure and pain. The virtual reality it generates is every bit as good as the real thing, better for all you know, except that it isn't the real thing. Perhaps you have never experienced the real thing, except very briefly when you were too young to remember, before the brain that you are now was extracted from the body that you had, from the skull that you had, like a walnut from its shell.

If we were on a different philosophical tack we could raise a lot of ethical questions about the terrible way in which you've been treated and your basic human rights disrespected, but our philosophical course is strictly epistemological at the moment.

The brain in a vat scenario is rather old hat these days; as is using the phrase 'old hat' to describe something old-fashioned or worn out. Younger philosophy students – that's anyone below the age of 40 – tend to cite *The Matrix* scenario instead of the brain in a vat scenario when playing the doubting game. *The Matrix* scenario is similar to the brain in a vat scenario, but rather than a brain in a vat experiencing a computer generated virtual or simulated reality, it involves legions of whole human bodies in vats experiencing a computer generated virtual or simulated reality. In case you don't know, perhaps because you live on the dark side of the moon or have a deep aversion to science fiction – people who like philosophy tend to like science fiction – *The Matrix* is a first rate science fiction-action movie released in 1999, written and directed by Larry and Andy Wachowski and starring Keanu Reeves, Laurence Fishburne and Carrie-Anne Moss.

The movie and its sequels have obtained cult status among sci-fi freaks, cyberpunks, hackers, goths, stoners and philosophy teachers. Philosophy teachers love the movie because it helps them to explain various complex philosophical themes to students by providing an accessible, exciting but nonetheless thoughtful illustration of those themes. They also love the movie because showing the whole director's cut DVD makes for a couple of very easy Friday afternoon lessons.

The movie reveals a world in which humans created artificial intelligence, sentient machines. The sentient machines, being on the whole smarter, more organized and less given to fatigue, have taken over the planet. Industry has scorched the sky, blocked out the sun, preventing the use of solar power as an energy source. Having no morals, the sentient machines have decided to use humans as a mere means. They grow them on vast farms for the electro-chemical energy their bodies produce. Each human body, or battery, is stored in a vat or pod of nutrient and is connected to an energy grid by tubes and wires. The nutrient is a soup made from the liquefied dead – all very efficient and self-sufficient. No other battery looks like it or lasts like it but the one drawback in this master plan is that the humans can't simply be kept in comas. Their minds have to be stimulated or their bodies perish.

To solve this problem, the sentient machines have created the matrix, a vast, computer generated, simulated reality that resembles in every detail the late twentieth century, the height of human civilization before the machines took over. Every human brain is plugged directly into the matrix via a deep single pin socket in the back of the head. Ouch! At first the matrix presented a perfect world but that didn't work. The humans failed to be fooled by complete happiness and fulfilment. They didn't know how to handle it or what to do with it and their minds kept waking up to the horror of their bodily situation. So the sentient machines created a challenging matrix, a simulated world defined by familiar, everyday human misery and suffering, and that worked much better.

A few human beings have avoided or escaped the machines and they free others from the vats who they think can most help their rebel cause. It's a hell of a shock for people to discover that it's closer to the year 2199 than 1999 and that the late-twentieth-century world of buildings, cars, juicy steaks and nightclubs isn't real; that it's just a matrix operated by merciless sentient machines who have been farming you and your kind for energy. Not surprisingly, some people never get over the shock, they want to forget everything and be plugged straight back into the matrix without delay. They are like the people in Plato's simile of the cave we considered earlier. The light of reality and truth overwhelms and terrifies them and they want nothing more than to crawl back into unreality and blissful ignorance.

The very philosophically minded comedian, Woody Allen, once wrote, 'Cloquet hated reality but realised it was still the only place to get a good steak' (*Side Effects*, p. 13). Well, in the world according to *The Matrix*, the matrix is the only place to get a good steak, all be it a simulated cyber-steak served with microchips. But then, as at least one character points out, a real steak and a perfectly simulated steak taste exactly the same. And if they don't, and you've never had real steak, then how can you make the comparison anyway? There are, of course, no steaks outside the matrix, or potato chips, or any other decent grub, just a grey, tasteless protein gruel. In fact, in 'the desert of the real' outside the matrix, on a sun starved planet dominated by mean machines, there isn't much of anything pleasant except the vivacious Trinity (Carrie-Anne Moss). As Morpheus (Laurence Fishburne) says to Neo (Keanu Reeves) as he offers him a choice between the red pill that will reveal the reality of his situation and the blue pill that will give him unquestioning faith in the make-believe world of the matrix, 'Remember, all I'm offering is the truth, nothing more.' How very much like the study of philosophy is taking that red pill.

The Matrix raises so many more philosophical questions than just those concerning the existence and nature of the external world, questions concerning human evolution, artificial intelligence, self-belief, truth, freedom, morality, hope, despair and fate, that it leads me to digress. I first saw this excellent movie at the end of a party where a certain amount of consciousness raising had already taken place, but I think it would have blown my mind anyway. If you haven't already seen it, definitely check it out. You might even want to read one or more of the many books that have been written on *The Matrix* and philosophy, such as *Taking the Red Pill: Science, Philosophy and Religion in The Matrix* by David Gerrold or *The Matrix and Philosophy: Welcome to the Desert of the Real* by William Irwin. These are just a couple of the titles available in what appears to be a small industry. When you've read them all, perhaps you could write one yourself. Always room for one more.

Yet another scenario my philosophy students are fond of citing when playing the doubting game is the *Red Dwarf: Back to Reality* scenario.

Again, if you live on the dark side of the moon or avoid anything vaguely sci-fi like the plague, then you may not have heard of the *Red Dwarf* sci-fi situation comedy written by Rob Grant and Doug Naylor. It features four space drifters, Lister the last human, Rimmer a hologramatic human, Cat a humanoid cat and Kryten a service mechanoid. These dysfunctional but remarkably resourceful misfits are lost in space aboard the 6 miles long, 5 miles tall and 4 miles wide mining spaceship, Red Dwarf. For those among you who are not astronomers, a red dwarf is a relatively small, relatively cool, low mass star.

The hugely popular eight series of *Red Dwarf* ran on the BBC between 1988 and 1999 and are now continually repeated on minor digital channels late at night. They are well worth watching if you don't mind your flow of comedy and profundity being constantly interrupted by commercials. Probably better to get the DVDs. Every philosophy teacher looking for those easy Friday afternoon lessons has the complete collectors' box set.

Apart from being hilariously funny with some superb one liners, *Red Dwarf* cleverly explores a wide range of philosophical themes. It is certainly as wide ranging in its philosophizing as *The Matrix*, which it may well have influenced. It is interesting, perhaps, that the last *Red Dwarf* series ended in 1999, the year *The Matrix* was released. If you are interested in getting hold of *Back to Reality*, or like me you are just an anorak who likes to have all the facts, it is the sixth and final episode of *Red Dwarf*, Series 5.

For most of the episode, *Back to Reality* has the same 'rude awakening' theme as *The Matrix*, with the four central characters emerging simultaneously from a total immersion computer simulation into a stark and hostile reality. Lister, Rimmer, Cat and Kryten are shocked to discover that their tolerably pleasant, adventurous life as the outlandish crew of the spaceship Red Dwarf was a mere illusion. The world they find themselves in is a bleak and brutal totalitarian state. The game is over, the space travelling existence that defined them has gone, and without it they no longer know who they are.

Each character falls into despair and loses the will to live as he discovers he is the kind of person he despises. Rimmer, once so fussy and self-important, finds he is a scruffy, alcoholic dropout who can no longer blame his parents for his failings. Lister, who prided himself on being a good man of moral courage, finds he is a murdering section chief of the totalitarian state. Kryten soon breaks the primary directive of his mechanoid existence by killing a man while Cat loses his cool, his looks and his dress sense.

They are about to commit suicide when the computer aboard Red Dwarf finally manages to snap them out of their collective nightmare and welcomes them back to reality. It turns out they have imagined emerging from a computer game into a bleak totalitarian state. It was all an hallucination brought on by the hallucinogenic, despair inducing ink venom of a giant despair squid.

This classic episode of *Red Dwarf* questions our certainty about what is real. It has us believing that what we thought was real was only a simulation or dream, only to reveal later on that the waking up was actually a falling asleep. The Red Dwarf crew is understandably relieved to discover that they are, after all, the Red Dwarf crew, but how do they know for sure? Perhaps they are not the Red Dwarf crew. Perhaps four individuals are in an artificial reality suite somewhere else being led to believe they have just recovered from an hallucination that led them to believe they were no longer the Red Dwarf crew.

Many philosophers argue that there is no way of knowing for sure that the world you think you're in right now isn't a dream. And if it suddenly seems you're waking up from the dream you can't in fact know for sure you're not falling asleep. Maybe you're dreaming all of it while floating in a reality you've never experienced. Confused? I'm beginning to confuse myself here, as well as give myself a bewildering sense of unreality, but the general point is that you can't ever know for absolute certain what is real. The very term 'reality' becomes so slippery that it is impossible to keep a firm hold on it or know what it really refers to.

The Buddhists put it all rather poetically when they say it is quite possible that at this very moment you may be a butterfly dreaming you are a human being. But if you suddenly wake up to find yourself fluttering around the cabbages on a summer morning trying to avoid being eaten by birds, how do you know you are not really a human being that has suddenly started dreaming it is a butterfly? Perhaps you noted the possibility that you are a butterfly dreaming it is a human, or something very similar, for the doubting exercise. Don't forget the doubting exercise. You are still doing it as you sit reading this book, or as you flutter around the cabbages imagining you are reading this book.

Solipsism – is there anything out there?

So far the focus has been on particular things that appear to be out there not being out there, and on the world that appears to be out there being very different from the world that is really out there. In other words, all the doubts considered so far assume that there is an external world of some sort, that there is something out there, some reality or other outside your mind, even if, like the brain in the vat or the vast majority of humans in *The Matrix* who never get freed from the pods, you are completely out of touch with that hidden reality and always will be. But perhaps there is no reality out there. Perhaps there is nothing at all outside your own mind! I don't mean an infinite void of space, I mean absolutely nothing at all whatsoever, naught, nil, zilch, zip, sweet FA. (It's hard to imagine nothing, perhaps because there is nothing to imagine.) Perhaps you are not even a brain in a vat or a cerebellum in a bucket. Perhaps you are just a non-physical, disembodied mind dreaming that the world exists.

This, of course, amounts to saying that your mind is the only thing, the only entity, that there is, the entire universe. It amounts to saying that the so-called external world, absolutely all of it, including what you are reading now, is just a figment of your very fertile imagination. In a sense, it amounts to saying you are God. In this scenario even your body is a figment of your imagination, an illusion, the stuff of dreams. Your head, your skull, your brain, do not really exist, just your ghostly, ethereal, intangible, incorporeal, brainless thoughts. Philosophers – or the philosophers you imagine exist – have a word for this: 'solipsism'.

'Solipsism' is derived from the Latin words *sōlus* (alone) and *ipse* (self). 'Solipsism' literally means *self-alone-ism*. It is the philosophical theory that one's own mind is the only thing that exists. Solipsism is just about the deepest depth of philosophical doubt a philosopher can dive down to; it is the Marianas Trench of scepticism. The only deeper doubt is doubting the existence of your own mind, although that might not in fact be possible. We'll look at doubting the existence of your own mind when we look at the philosophy of Descartes.

However ridiculous and extreme the problem of solipsism may seem, many philosophers have argued that it is strictly irrefutable. This does not mean that it is certainly the case, simply that it can't be dismissed beyond doubt as a possibility. Quite simply, if I must have a mind in order to have impressions of the world and my impressions of the world are impressions in my mind, it seems I can never prove there is a world giving rise to my impressions. There seems to be no getting away from the possibility that these so-called impressions might correspond to nothing at all and be entirely self-generated. Other philosophers, Descartes for example, have attempted to refute solipsism, to dismiss and overcome it, to prove that it is not the case. We will look at Descartes' views shortly.

Interestingly, although this is not a disproof of solipsism, it is psychologically impossible to really believe in solipsism. That is, it is impossible to *be* a solipsist, to act as though solipsism is the case. Suppose, as a philosopher, I decided solipsism is true. How would I then live in accordance with that belief? What would I do with myself? How would I conduct myself and my relationships with other people? If I was certain there are no other people, there would be no point writing books to convince them that solipsism is the case. Even the book itself, as far as I was concerned, would be nothing independent of me, just an idea or collection of ideas in my mind.

There is an amusing anecdote philosophy teachers like to tell philosophy students at this point to further illustrate the argument and enliven proceedings. It is not the kind of anecdote that has them rolling in the aisles, but neither is it so unfunny that it produces an awkward silence punctuated only by the sound of a funeral bell tolling in the distance. Anyway, there was once a philosophically minded gentleman who, after long deliberations, became convinced that solipsism is the case. He enthusiastically declared himself to be a solipsist and began attending philosophy conferences around the world for the purpose of meeting other solipsists and sharing his views with them.

Actually, this amusing anecdote, which philosophy teachers alter and embroider in accordance with the intelligence, attention span and sense of humour of their students, has its origins in a letter once received by the twentieth-century British philosopher, pacifist and womanizer, Bertrand Russell. Russell later wrote about the letter in a book he called, *Human Knowledge: Its Scope and Limits.* Russell writes:

> As against solipsism it is to be said, in the first place, that it is psychologically impossible to believe, and is rejected in fact even by those who mean to accept it. I once received a letter from an eminent logician, Mrs. Christine Ladd Franklin, saying that she was a solipsist, and was surprised that there were no others. Coming from a logician, this surprise surprised me. (p. 161)

I can entertain the philosophical view that solipsism is the case. I can definitely hold on quite strong philosophical grounds that it is an irrefutable possibility. I will, nonetheless, totally reject solipsism and affirm a practical belief in the existence of the external world and other people with everything I say and do.

While I've been writing this section, workmen have been cutting the grass verges along my road. Mowers, strimmers and grass blowers have all been blasting away at my concentration with alarmingly high decibels. Even if I considered myself a solipsist, surely I could not fail to be irritated by the noise, to wish the workmen would quickly finish and go away. And, surely, my irritation and my wishes affirm that I believe the external world exists as something independent of me.

A possible objection to this is that I can believe the mowers, the noise, the workmen are all just thoughts in my mind. I can nonetheless be irritated by these thoughts and wish them to be replaced by quieter thoughts. Even if everything is just thoughts in my mind it doesn't follow that I should somehow have control over these thoughts. But then, if I have no control over these thoughts at all, they already seem to have a certain independence from me, a certain objectivity. Perhaps the workmen are just *ideas* in my mind, but not, so to speak, *my* ideas. But then if they are not my ideas and I have no control over them – I can't, for example, make the workmen vanish simply by wishing it – then these ideas must have come from some other source, God perhaps. Now, if God is responsible for the ideas in my mind that create the appearance of an external world, then solipsism is definitely false because something exists other than my own mind, namely God.

The view that there is no material world but instead an infinite collection of ideas created by God is a version of what is called *idealism*. The most famous proponent of this version of idealism is the eighteenth-century Irish philosopher, theologian and Bishop of Cloyne, George Berkeley. In fact, this form of idealism is so closely associated with Berkeley that it is generally known as *Berkeleyan idealism*. Berkeley argues that there are no material things, only collections of ideas that are perceived by the mind.

According to his friend and biographer, James Boswell, when asked what he thought of Berkeleyan idealism, Dr Samuel 'Dictionary' Johnson famously kicked a stone and hurt his foot saying, 'I refute it thus' (*Life of Johnson*, p. 333). Berkeley, of course, would have replied that Johnson's foot, the pain in Johnson's foot and the stone were all just ideas in Johnson's mind. According to Berkeley, ideas exist only in so far as they are perceived by the mind. He argues that *to be is to be perceived*, or as he puts it in what has become one of the most famous maxims in philosophy, *esse est percipi* (*Principles of Human Knowledge*, Pt 1). The really big one liners in philosophy are almost always in Latin.

To prevent his theory from being indistinguishable from solipsism, Berkeley factors in the all important notion of God. 'Things' (i.e., collections of ideas), argues Berkeley, do not cease to exist when they are not being perceived by me because they are always perceived by an all seeing, all knowing, eternal God. In other words, an omniscient, omnipresent God continually thinks all those collections of ideas we call things and so prevents them from being merely *subjective* and from going out of existence when I'm not thinking them. God makes those collections of ideas we call things *objective*. He thinks all of them all the time. Not even Wikipedia can do that.

There is a limerick by the twentieth-century English theologian, priest and crime writer, Ronald Arbuthnott Knox, summarizing the philosophy of George Berkeley, in which a young man says that God must think it odd if a tree continues to exist when there is no one about. God replies to the young man in no uncertain terms that the tree will continue to exist 'Since observed by *Yours faithfully*, GOD'.

I've bounced rapidly around a lot of philosophical territory here just to give you a flavour of where thinking about the ins and outs of solipsism can lead. Like Berkeley, Descartes, who we will look at very shortly, also factors in the notion of God in an attempt to refute solipsism.

The psychological impossibility of belief in solipsism is revealed most clearly in my attitudes towards other people. If I genuinely believed that other people were just thoughts in my mind why would I love or hate them, want to share experiences with them and feel ashamed or proud in front of them and so on? Surely, it is not possible to relate to other people in all the complex psychological and emotional ways that I do in my everyday life while at the same time believing that they are mere figments of my imagination. This does not prove that other people exist, it simply shows that I have an unshakeable belief that they do, a belief that is not *stated* (except in weird books like this) but *lived*.

Ironically, it is only when philosophers try to prove that other people exist that doubts about their existence creep in. Sartre says, 'If I do not conjecture about the Other, then, precisely, I affirm him' (*Being and Nothingness*, p. 275). And expressing the same thought as Sartre, Wittgenstein says, 'My attitude towards him is an attitude towards a soul. I am not of the *opinion* that he has a soul' (*Philosophical Investigations*, iv, p. 178). Wittgenstein and Sartre hit the nail on the head here, as they so often do. Like Mrs Christine Ladd Franklin I can form the philosophical *opinion* that solipsism is the case while sitting alone in my study cogitating, but I will nonetheless maintain the *attitude* that other people exist, an attitude that will be revealed the moment my wife barges into my study with a cup of tea and a biscuit and disturbs my self-indulgent train of thought.

Although philosophical sceptics may well be quite right to insist that the existence of other people can't be proven, that there is no refuting what is known as the *problem of other minds*, even the philosophical sceptic will find himself continually affirming the existence of other people in the way he behaves and experiences himself as shy, proud, embarrassed, ashamed or in love when other people appear on the scene.

I have now said more than enough about solipsism for you to get the following joke, as well as recognize how bad it is:

Question: Why was the solipsist unhappy?
Answer: Because no one would accept his arguments as valid.

Maybe that should be, 'because there was no one to accept his arguments as valid' . . . Whatever.

Well, that just about wraps up the doubting exercise that we began way back. I've gone through just about every reason for doubting the existence of the external world or parts of it that I can think of. My philosophy students, or what appeared to me to be my philosophy students at the time I believed I was teaching them, have suggested all these possibilities over the years and I'm confident that you managed to think of similar possibilities yourself.

The father of modern philosophy

I will now, as promised, look at Descartes and his philosophy. His philosophy not only brilliantly organizes and encapsulates all that has been said so far in this chapter, it attempts to overcome many of the doubts that have been raised. Although Descartes obviously didn't draw upon such riches as *Red Dwarf* and *The Matrix*, since the start of this chapter we have been more or less reinventing a wheel first invented by Descartes way back in the seventeenth century. I don't apologize for forcing you to reinvent the Cartesian wheel because I'm sure you've learnt a lot from the exercise. After all, this book is called *How to be a Philosopher*, not *Yet Another Boring Introduction to Descartes*. Having played the same doubting game as Descartes played several centuries ago, it is very likely that you are now far more interested in how Descartes played the game himself and the conclusions he reached than you would have been had I simply started by banging on about some crusty, long dead French philosopher who suffered in cold weather, was often ill and spent most of his time in bed.

René Descartes (pronounced 'Decar') was born in 1596 in a small French town called La Haye en Touraine. In 1802 the town was renamed la Haye Descartes in his honour and in 1967 this was shortened to just Descartes. If you become a famous philosopher maybe they'll name a town after you, although you'll probably have to be dead a couple of hundred years before they do it. If you find that you particularly like Descartes you might even want to make a pilgrimage to Descartes. I recently made a sort of pilgrimage to the grave of Jean-Paul Sartre and Simone de Beauvoir at Montparnasse Cemetery in Paris. They are buried together, which means you can kill two dead philosophers with one headstone, so to speak. Anyway, where were we? Descartes, the town and the man.

Descartes was a sickly child who defied everyone's expectations including his own by not dying young. At the age of 8 he entered a Jesuit college where he had his own room and was allowed to get up when he liked. This was the start of Descartes' famous life-long habit of reading and writing in bed before he finally got up at 11 a.m. When Descartes was finally forced to break this habit in 1650 by Queen Christina of Sweden, who demanded he give her philosophy lessons at 5 a.m., it pretty soon killed him. If one of those smug, sanctimonious fogies whose chief virtue in life is rising before dawn ever tells you that getting up early never did anyone any harm, tell them it destroyed Descartes, one of the finest minds in the history of the world.

I seem to have inadvertently killed Descartes off without saying anything about the intervening years. Well, not surprisingly, he travelled a fair bit, built up his reputation by writing various influential texts, associated with various rich and powerful people, managed to avoid others who took offence at some of his more radical ideas, grew his hair long and did one or two scandalous things. Those of you who like a bit of soap opera with your philosophy will be interested to know that he had an illegitimate daughter called Francine who died at the age of 5. Descartes was heartbroken.

The main thing about Descartes, as with all great philosophers, is that he was extremely clever. He was particularly good at mathematics and geometry and made his name as a mathematician before he branched out into philosophy. He always saw maths and philosophy as pretty closely connected, as many philosophers do. Maths reveals, or appears to reveal, a higher world of certainty that *rationalist* philosophers like Descartes view as more real than the imperfect, empirical world we encounter through our senses. Descartes is still respected as a major mathematician and, as the mathematicians among you will know, his theories are still studied to this day in school maths lessons around the world.

He was such a good mathematician that one of his hobbies was sending other famous mathematicians problems they couldn't solve. He deliberately presented the problems in the most obscure manner his cunning mind could invent, just to make things even more tricky. It was the fashion of the day to wrap the truth up in codes, anagrams and puzzles and make it all seem rather Dan Brown and magical, but Descartes also liked to scoff at his mathematical contemporaries when they failed to work the problems out. This perhaps reveals a more unpleasant, spiteful, stuck-up side to the sickly little man. On the other hand, he may have liked to baffle other intellectuals because he thought it was they who were stuck-up.

While he liked to flummox the intellectual elite of scholars, pedants and priests, he was very keen to make his ideas accessible to a growing population of educated middle-class folk who were characterized by their open-mindedness and common sense rather than by theological and academic prejudice. To this end he often wrote in French rather than scholarly Latin, a somewhat vulgar thing to do at the time. He once remarked that one of his most important works, *Discourse on Method*, was written in such away that even women could understand it. As the philosopher Bernard Williams points out in his excellent book, *Descartes: The Project of Pure Enquiry*, this was a comment on the reading habits of the time rather than a sexist statement (*Descartes: The Project of Pure Enquiry*, footnote 5, p. 19). After all, Descartes died teaching philosophy to a woman.

Descartes is the subject of possibly the worst joke in the history of philosophy.

Question: How do philosophers get about?
Answer: In de car.

Interestingly, there is some truth in this awful joke in that many philosophers since Descartes have made progress in their careers on the back of Descartes. That is to say, the stock in trade of much of philosophy since Descartes has been to interpret, analyse and criticize Descartes. To unpack him, gut him, pick him apart, overturn him, reassemble him and generally give him a right good mauling.

Descartes is widely known as 'the father of modern philosophy' – philosophy moves so slowly that it considers 1592 as modern – because it was he who raised most of the questions and issues that have preoccupied, perplexed and inspired philosophy ever since. He also introduced, or rather reintroduced from the ancient Greeks, the sceptical method of philosophizing so favoured by Socrates and Plato which we ourselves have been practicing in this chapter. Above all, he showed that philosophizing, rather than begin with accepting certain claims on the basis of authority, can and should begin with the individual intellect confronting the mystery of existence without preconceptions or prejudices and asking, 'What is this existence, what am I in relation to it and what can I know for sure about it all?' Bernard Williams says that after Descartes there was 'no question of a return to authority'. Williams goes on to say: 'Nothing will be rationally believed because it was discovered by Descartes, even if it takes Descartes to discover it. It will be believed because, when put before the unprejudiced mind, it compels consent by its own rational clarity' (*Descartes: The Project of Pure Enquiry*, p. 30).

Descartes' towering achievement as a philosopher was to ask precisely the philosophical questions he asked at precisely the point in history when he asked them. The new sciences of physics, astronomy, chemistry and so on were spreading their wings and struggling to soar beyond astrology and alchemy and a lot of other hocus-pocus. It is a sign of how backward things were in Descartes' time that witch-burning was still a favourite pursuit of the church. The new sciences needed philosophy to indicate the firmest foundation for take off, to point the way, to instruct them on the best general methods of reasoning to follow and to reassure them that certain knowledge of the physical world was possible. But philosophy had lost its own way, making little or no progress as it turned the same old tight theological circles, appealing to the authority of the ancients, particularly Aristotle, to settle every dispute. Aristotle, like Descartes, was a towering genius, but it didn't mean something was right just because Aristotle said so.

Descartes threw a reviving bucket of cold water over philosophy and dragged it out of the ditch where it had been snoring in a drunken, religious stupor for far too long. He dusted it down, got the smudges off its craggy old face with spit on a handkerchief, tied a shiny new pair of sceptical boots to its worn feet and sent it trudging on its miserable way. Ok, so it staggered up a few blind alleys at first, it still staggers up blind alleys quite often – it doesn't know they are blind until it gets up them – but thanks to Descartes it has a *method* that is always prepared to question authority and expert opinion as it searches for the truth. It has the reverse gear of scepticism that always allows it to back up, all be it with painful, grinding slowness, out of each and every cul-de-sac it invents for itself.

Descartes' masterpiece, the work that epitomizes his philosophy and most clearly exhibits his sceptical method, his *method of doubt*, is his *Meditations on First Philosophy* published in 1641. It is in this work that Descartes so brilliantly draws together, organizes and summarizes the key ideas we were kicking around earlier while playing the doubting game. As I said a few paragraphs ago, in so many words, Descartes shows that philosophizing must begin with the individual, unprejudiced intellect raising fundamental questions about itself and the world. This approach is at the very heart of the *Meditations*.

To read the *Meditations* is not to be subjected to the authority of Descartes' scholarly opinions, but rather to start philosophizing from scratch along with Descartes. Each person who reads the *Meditations* is encouraged to be Descartes, to doubt everything, including his own existence, before he strives to cure himself of his doubts with a strong dose of cold, hard reason. As I tell my long-suffering students when we study the *Meditations*, 'This book is not about Descartes, it is about each individual who reads it. Each one of us is Descartes – doubting, striving for certainty, philosophizing.' Well, I don't actually say all this. I just tend to say, smacking the book passionately, desperately, 'Don't you see, we are all Descartes!'

Anyway, if I stop banging on and just explain what goes on in the *Meditations* you will hopefully see what I mean. Don't treat this summary as a substitute for reading the *Meditations*, however. Good philosophers are well read, even if they refuse to accept anything simply on the basis of authority.

Descartes and the method of doubt

Descartes famously begins his *Meditations* by saying that from his earliest years he has 'accepted many false opinions as being true' (*I Med*, p. 95) and that he has built up a 'doubtful and uncertain' (*I Med*, p. 95) belief system on the basis of his false opinions. For a long time he has planned to sit down and have a good hard think about these false opinions and try to rid himself of them once and for all. What with one thing and another, however – illness, travelling, teaching, lounging around in bed – he has just never gotten around to it. He also says he needed to be old enough, 'sufficiently mature' (*I Med*, p. 95), to do the job properly. At last the time has come. There will never be a better time. His mind is 'free from all cares' (*I Med*, p. 95) and he has obtained for himself, probably by finally scraping enough money together, 'assured leisure in peaceful solitude' (*I Med*, p. 95).

Anyone who has ever struggled to find the time and opportunity to do some really serious work in philosophy will know exactly what Descartes means. Philosophy isn't that hard, it's finding the peace and quiet and the ocean of open-ended time required to do it that is hard. Even as I write, a car alarm goes off nearby. A thousand curses on the inventor of the car alarm for the myriad fine threads of philosophical thought you've broken. At least Descartes didn't have to contend with car alarms, police sirens, helicopters, ghetto blasters and 'this vehicle is reversing' beepers. Just the sound of horses' hooves and the screams of innocent women burning.

Perfectly ready, Descartes says, 'I shall apply myself seriously and freely to the general destruction of all my former opinions' (*I Med*,

p. 95), and so off he goes and does just that. Employing what has come to be known as the *method of doubt*, he undertakes to doubt every opinion he holds, for whatever reason he can think of, in the hope of discovering at the bottom of it all an opinion that just can't be doubted, an opinion that can withstand whatever doubts he throws at it. If he can find such an indubitable opinion, this will serve as a firm and reliable foundation for rebuilding the edifice of knowledge. As well as being described as a rationalist and a sceptic, Descartes is also often described as a *foundationalist*. His project as a philosopher is to tear down the dull, rickety, decaying structure of uncertain knowledge using the wrecking ball of doubt; so that, on the firm foundation he hopes to expose at the end of the demolition process, he and others can begin to construct a clean, bright, sturdy skyscraper of certainty.

Each of the doubts Descartes raises in his method of doubt is more serious than the last. He tends to raise a doubt, followed by a reservation that suggests the doubt is perhaps not so bad after all, before moving on to a more serious doubt that pulls the rug out from under whatever 'certainty' he thought he'd just got hold of. His doubts can be seen as representing different levels of doubt, each one deeper and more fundamental than the last. At each stage of the process he exposes what he has long assumed he knew for certain to be just another poorly founded belief. At each stage the wrecking ball of doubt swings into action and knocks the poorly founded belief aside.

Like many philosophers before him, stretching way back to the ancient Greeks, the first thing Descartes doubts is the reliability of his senses – his powers of sight, smell, touch, taste and hearing. 'I have sometimes found that these senses played me false,' he says, 'and it is prudent never to trust those who have once deceived us' (*I Med*, p. 96). We have all mistaken a distant bush for a man, heard a voice at our ear when there was nobody there, thought a tower was falling on us when it was only the clouds moving or our body swaying. When we are ill or on drugs we sometimes hallucinate – a lot has already been said about hallucination – while familiar foods have an unusual taste and smell or no taste and smell at all. Apparently, to people suffering from jaundice everything looks as yellow as they do. What if we all suffered from jaundice all the time, would the general belief be that the word was tinted yellow?

I have some cycling goggles that make everything look yellow. I don't wear them. My senses are unreliable enough without further confusing the situation. And who hasn't seen those optical illusions in psychology books in which lines of the same length appear to be different lengths and patterns appear to swirl on a static page? You only have to hold your finger close in front of your face and alternately close one eye as you open the other. As you will see, you finger moves from left to right and back again. Each of your eyes is telling you your finger is in a different place. So where exactly is your finger? Can you absolutely rely on your eyes to tell you this? Put your hand in a bucket of cold water. You call it cold and your senses tell you it's cold. But put your hand in the freezer for a while – don't get frostbite – then shove it back in the bucket. The so-called cold water is now warm water. So is it cold water or warm water? Can you trust your senses to tell you what temperature the water really is?

Descartes' reservation to all this scepticism about the reliability of the senses is that some sensations seem to be much clearer and far more reliable than others. It is easy to mistake a distant bush for a man at sunset when the light is fading and the shadows grow long, but surely not so easy to make mistakes regarding what I perceive to be right in front of me on this desk in sharp electric light when I'm wide awake, healthy and sober. As Descartes says:

> But, although the senses sometimes deceive us, concerning things which are barely perceptible or at a great distance, there are perhaps many other things about which one cannot reasonably doubt, although we know them through the medium of the senses, for example, that I am here, sitting by the fire, wearing a dressing-gown, with this paper in my hands, and other things of this nature. (*I Med*, p. 96)

Pulling the rug out from under this reservation as he dives to a deeper level of doubt (it is amazing he can move at all, I have so ensnared him in mixed metaphors), Descartes makes the point that he has often dreamt that he was sitting by the fire in his dressing-gown when he was actually in bed. 'How many times have I dreamt at night that I was in this place, dressed, by the fire, although I was quite naked in my bed' (*I Med*, p. 96). It's official, Descartes slept in the nude! That's surprising. I have always imagined him as a nightgown and sleeping cap kind of a guy. A Wee Willie Winkie of a philosopher, propped up against a stack of pillows writing his *Meditations*. 'I see so clearly,' he writes, 'that there are no conclusive signs by means of which one can distinguish clearly between being awake and being asleep' (*I Med*, p. 97). In short, it is always possible at any moment that he is dreaming.

Never mind how reliable or unreliable his senses are, it is possible that none of his experiences is ever the product of sensory perception, possible that it is all an illusion, possible that he is dreaming he has a body with sense organs attached, possible that in reality no such object exists at all.

Remember, Descartes is doubting with the ultimate aim of finding something undoubtable and at this point he expresses the reservation that even if it is all a dream the basic elements that comprise the dream are nonetheless, in an important sense, real and reliable. Red is still red even in a dream and can't also be blue. Dreams may be weird and wonderful, as the world we seem to perceive is weird and wonderful, but it all accords to a certain basic logic. Even in a dream, two pink elephants and two pink elephants make four pink elephants and triangles have no more or less than three sides. I can't dream a six-sided square or a monster with two heads that only has one head. As Descartes says:

And by the same reasoning, although these general things, viz. eyes, head, hands and the like, may be imaginary, we have to admit that there are even simpler and more universal things which are true and exist, from the mixture of which, no more or less than from the mixture of certain real colours, all the images of things, whether true and real or fictitious and fantastic, which dwell in our thoughts, are formed. . . . For whether I am awake or sleeping, two and three added together always make five, and a square never has more than four sides; and it does not seem possible that truths so apparent can be suspected of any falsity or uncertainty. (*I Med*, pp. 97–8)

Does the logicality or logicalness of the basic numerical, geometrical and colour elements of the objects of his thoughts, his dreams, provide Descartes with the certainty he is looking for? You might think that as a mathematician he would happily settle on the logic, the lack of contradiction that is displayed even in dreams, as the indubitable truth he is looking for. You might think that he would seize upon logic and maths as the firm bedrock on which to begin building the sturdy, reliable skyscraper of certain knowledge, but he doesn't. He casts doubt even upon logic and maths, questioning their apparently undeniable certainty with a doubt that is so utterly deep it plumbs the absolute pits and bowels of philosophical scepticism. Descartes supposes that an 'evil demon, no less cunning and deceiving than powerful' (*I Med*, p. 100) fools him every time he makes a judgement about anything whatsoever. The evil demon, also known as the evil genius or Descartes' demon, not only fools him into believing that he is sensing a world that does not actually exist, it fools him every time he makes a judgement based on seemingly rock solid logical and mathematical principles. In this way Descartes casts doubt, all be it a rather contrived doubt, even on the certainty of basic logic. It is impossible to conceive how 2+2 could equal anything else but 4 or how the evil demon fools him into thinking that 2+2=4 if it doesn't, but there we are. That is the doubt Descartes raises. He invites us to accept, for argument's sake, that this is a possible doubt.

Descartes flirts with the idea that it is God who deceives him, even daring to suppose, temporarily and for mere argument's sake, that there is no God, but he has to tread very carefully for fear of being accused of heresy. Remember, while Descartes was penning the

Meditations there were still lots of crazy Christians stomping about who loved to spit-roast heretics. So, out of fear and respect for the church, he went with the evil demon argument instead. Despite his caution, his ideas still made him enemies and he thought it best to quit France in favour of relatively liberal Holland.

Some commentators argue that Descartes was too concerned about offending the church. Far more outspoken philosophers remained in Paris, some of them even daring to endorse the heretical Copernican theory that the Earth is not at the centre of the universe, and they didn't get roasted – well, not all of them anyway. What should not be forgotten is that although Descartes was a radical thinker for his time, he sincerely believed in God, genuinely respected religion and wanted his writings to be accepted by the conservative establishment for purposes of education and instruction. One of the main aims of the *Meditations* is to reconcile philosophy and science with religion, to show that they need not be opposed but can in fact clarify and support one another. As you will see shortly, Descartes proceeds to offer a proof of the existence of God, then attempts to use this proof as a basis for certainty about the existence of the external world. Right now, however, Descartes is not certain about anything.

Philosophical doubt has annihilated Descartes' world, his dressing-gown, his body, even his former confidence in the certainty of maths and logic. By the end of his *First Mediation* and at the start of his *Second Meditation* he is so mired in a thick, steaming quagmire of doubt that it is poised to suck him under for ever. As he sinks to his chin in the quicksand, he wonders if the only thing that is certain is that nothing in the world is certain:

> I suppose therefore that all the things I see are false; I persuade myself that none of those things ever existed that my deceptive memory represents to me; I suppose I have no senses; I believe that body, figure, extension, movement and place are only fictions of my mind. What then, shall be considered true? Perhaps only this, that there is nothing certain in the world. (*II Med*, p. 102)

Descartes, 'I think therefore I am' and God

Remarkably, with his last ounce of strength Descartes forces a muddy hand out of the quagmire and firmly grasps an overhanging branch. It is little more than a twig really, but incredibly strong, if not unbreakable. It is the certainty he has been looking for, the one he had all but lost hope of finding, and he will use this fixed point to pull himself clean out of the swamp of uncertainty.

The certainty that Descartes snatches from the jaws of all-consuming doubt is his inability to doubt that he exists, at least as a thinking thing. The more he doubts himself the more he affirms his existence as a thinking thing by the very fact that he doubts. Why? Because to doubt is to think. As he says, 'There is therefore no doubt that I exist, if he [the evil demon] deceives me; and let him deceive me as much as he likes, he can never cause me to be nothing, so long as I think I am something' (*II Med*, p. 103).

As you may already know, this argument is very well summed up by the single most famous sound-bite in the entire history of philosophy: 'I think, therefore I am' (*Discourse on Method, IV*, p. 53). It is so famous that even its Latin translation, *Cogito ergo sum*, is famous; the only bit of Latin most people know besides *et cetera* and *curriculum vitae*. Note that this great one-liner is not found in the *Meditations* as you might expect but in the *Discourse on Method*. I wonder how many poor souls since the seventeenth century have scoured the *Meditations* searching in vain for Descartes' great maxim. Not many actually, as almost anyone who has ever taught Descartes' philosophy has added a flourish to their lecture by knowledgeably pointing out that the line which best sums up the most important argument in Descartes' *Meditations* is not in Descartes' *Meditations*.

However you imagine it, a branch a man grasps to save himself from drowning, a fixed point, a firm foundation, 'I think therefore I am' is so solid and certain that in Descartes' view it will serve as the basis for constructing a sturdy edifice of *knowledge* to replace the shaky edifice of uncertain beliefs he has just demolished. As a master of mathematical and logical deduction, Descartes is cautiously optimistic that as long as he possesses one, absolute truth, and proceeds very carefully, he can deduce and work out other truths from it that are equally certain and reliable. His ultimate aim is to overcome solipsism by proving the existence of the external world. He wants to reclaim the external world having lost it in a fog of doubt earlier in his *Meditations*.

Confident that he *knows* he is a thing that thinks he quite sensibly undertakes to examine his thoughts to see what he can find there. What he finds is the idea of God, the idea of a supreme, infinite and perfect being. Crucially, he argues that he could not have made up this idea himself. It is too perfect for a finite, imperfect creature to conjure up on his own. So, it must have come from God. So, God must exist. Neat.

What we have here is a version of what is known as the Ontological Argument in which the very idea of God is supposed to imply God's existence. It dates back at least as far as the medieval philosopher, St Anselm, who argues in his *Proslogion* that it is not possible to think of God as not existing because the very idea of God is the idea of a supreme being who possesses all positive attributes, one of which must be existence. In other words, the most perfect conceivable entity must exist, otherwise it would lack that attribute and therefore not be perfect.

Descartes' twist on the Ontological Argument is to claim that God is the *cause* of Descartes' idea of him. This has come to be known as the Trademark Argument. As the supreme being, God is the creator and source of all things. Descartes is therefore God's creation and the idea of God that Descartes has in his mind is his creator's trademark, hallmark, stamp or brand.

Descartes' project is nothing if not ambitious. On his way to proving the external world, as a crucial step towards that proof, he offers us a proof of God's existence. Descartes' proof of the external world, his refutation of solipsism, follows in short order. God is perfect in every way, including morally perfect. He would not, therefore, deceive Descartes into thinking that there was an external world if there wasn't. So, the external world must really exist as it appears to and is not simply an illusion. For Descartes, God is no less than the guarantor of the existence of the external world. Again, very neat.

Descartes' collapse into solipsism

There is no doubt that what Descartes offers us is an ingenious series of arguments in order to try and prove the existence of the external world and overcome the solipsistic doubts that have haunted him and us throughout this chapter. Rejecting the direct, empirical, sensory route to the external world as unreliable (we can't trust our senses), in true rationalist style Descartes contrives a circuitous, a priori route via God. Circuitous, but nonetheless neat. Too neat, most critics say. Too many papered over cracks.

As mentioned earlier, the stock in trade of much of philosophy since Descartes has been to criticize Descartes, and certainly many of his ideas and arguments don't stand up to close scrutiny. It is beyond the scope of this book to look in detail at all the ways in which Descartes has been criticized and there are plenty of books already available that are dedicated to doing just that. It is important, however, to consider some of the main problems with the series of arguments by which he attempts to prove the existence of the external world, as it is that elusive external world that we are most concerned with here. At this point, in the interests of becoming a philosopher who thinks for him or herself, rather than simply being a sponge, you might want to pause a while before you read on and try to think for yourself what some of these problems are. . . .

To begin with, despite being just about the best candidate for certain, foundational knowledge that ever put on a suit and ran for office, there are various problems with 'I think therefore I am'. One of the main ones is, what does Descartes mean by 'I'? What is this underlying I, self or ego that has thoughts? Is its existence really so certain? Does the existence of thoughts imply the existence of a metaphysical self that has these thoughts? The empiricist philosopher, David Hume, later argued against Descartes and those rationalist philosophers who agreed with Descartes that there is no such thing as the self, only a series of sensory impressions and the ideas that are copies of those impressions. Nowhere in this flow of impressions and ideas is there to be found a fixed I or self that has them. Hume writes:

> If any impression gives rise to the idea of self, that impression must con-
> tinue invariably the same, thro' the whole course of our lives; since self is
> suppos'd to exist after that manner. But there is no impression constant
> and invariable. Pain and pleasure, grief and joy, passions and sensations
> succeed each other, and never all exist at the same time. It cannot, there-
> fore, be from any of these impressions, or from any other, that the idea of
> self is deriv'd; and consequently there is no such idea. . . . For my part,
> when I enter most intimately into what I call *myself*, I always stumble on
> some particular perception or other, of heat or cold, light or shade, love or
> hatred, pain or pleasure. I never catch *myself* at any time without a percep-
> tion, and never can observe any thing but the perception. (*A Treatise of
> Human Nature*, pp. 251–2)

The next set of problems relate to Descartes' claim that he has an idea of an infinite, perfect being. Descartes says he is certain he has an idea of such a being, that the idea was put there by the infinite, perfect being himself, but is it really possible to have such an idea? We know what the words 'infinite' and 'perfect' mean, or at least we know how to use these words, but is that the same as clearly conceiving infinity or perfection?

Arguably, infinity is inconceivable. Astronomers have detected a galaxy that is 13 billion light years away from Earth. That is, the light from that galaxy has travelled for 13 billion years across space at a speed of 186,000 miles per second to get here. It is impossible to really conceive of this awesome but nonetheless limited distance, to really get your head around it, so how much more impossible is it to conceive of an infinite distance or an infinite duration? As mathematicians point out, we can't think of an infinitely high number. However high the number we think of we can always add 1 to it, then 1 to that number and so on.

As for perfection, we use the word to describe a face, a meal or a day out but was the face, the meal or the day out truly perfect in the sense that it could not have been bettered at all? Can we conceive what would *truly* correspond to the word 'perfection' on earth or in heaven?

Some philosophers have argued that we only have ideas of finitude and imperfection. These are gained from our experience of a finite, imperfect world. My idea of perfection is not a true idea of perfection but only the idea of a lack of imperfection. Similarly, my idea of infinity is not a true idea of infinity but only the idea of a lack of limitation. So, it is only by negating my ideas of limited, imperfect things that I arrive at the semblance of an idea of an infinite, perfect being. I do not, as Descartes claims, have an idea of what God is, only an idea of what God is not.

Back in the mists of time, well, the 1980s, I was taught philosophy of religion by a very dignified former Dominican monk called Lubor Velecky who had taught at the Vatican College in Rome and helped to translate the complete works of St Thomas Aquinas into English. In an influential paper that he wrote, Velecky says, 'The divine creator is to be characterised in terms of denials of certain characteristics found in the world of our experience . . . we can not know what God is but only what he is not' ('The Five Ways: Proofs Of God's Existence?').

Even supposing Descartes has a clear idea of God, does the mere idea of God imply the existence of God as Descartes claims? In other words, does the famous Ontological Argument for the existence of God, first formulated by St Anselm and so popular with many medieval and later philosophers, actually work? The short answer to that question is no. That it doesn't work was noted by several philosophers prior to Descartes, including the great Catholic theologian, St Thomas Aquinas, who was smart enough to leave it out of his 'five ways' – his five proofs of God's existence. So, Descartes helped himself to an argument that was already well past its sell-by date even in 1641. So, what exactly is wrong with the Ontological Argument?

Suppose I said, 'The perfect singer has a perfect voice.' This is necessarily true in the sense that it is a contradiction to say, 'The perfect singer does not have a perfect voice.' How could the perfect singer be perfect if she had a voice that was not perfect? It belongs to the very *idea* of the perfect singer that she has a perfect voice. However, none of this implies that there is a perfect singer actually existing somewhere in the universe. Although it is necessarily true to say, 'The perfect singer has a perfect voice,' and a contradiction to say, 'The perfect singer does not have a perfect voice,' there is no contradiction if we reject the *entire* proposition. That the perfect singer must necessarily be judged to have a perfect voice does not mean that the perfect singer exists.

Now, 'God' means 'a being with all positive attributes'. By definition, 'God' means 'a being that is all powerful, all knowing, everywhere, infinite and so on'. Therefore, it is a contradiction to say, 'God is a being without all positive attributes.' How could an idea of God be an idea of God if it was the idea of something that was lacking in some way? It belongs to the very *idea* of God that he has all positive attributes including the attribute of existence. 'Exists' is an essential feature of the *idea* 'God'. However, none of this implies that God actually exists. 'Exists' is so much a part of the idea 'God' that the proposition, 'God does not exist', is a contradiction. But there is no contradiction if we reject the *entire* proposition, just as no contradiction remained when we rejected the *entire* contradictory proposition about the perfect singer not having a perfect voice.

This is undoubtedly one of the more complicated points in this book and you may have to go away and read more about the long history of the Ontological Argument from medieval to modern times in order to fully grasp why it doesn't work. Basically, the Ontological Argument makes an illegitimate move from saying, quite rightly, that some ideas logically imply other ideas – like the idea of the perfect singer implying the idea of a perfect voice – to saying, quite wrongly, that at least one idea logically implies that a certain thing exists. That it is possible to reason from one idea to another does not mean that it is possible to reason from the idea of a thing to the existence of that thing. As Kant puts it in his *Critique of Pure Reason*, in a section dedicated to showing the impossibility of an ontological proof of the existence of God, 'But the unconditioned necessity of a judgement is not the same as the absolute necessity of things' (*Critique of Pure Reason*, p. 501).

In dismissing the Ontological Argument, Bertrand Russell argues that existence cannot be included among the attributes or properties of a thing because saying that a thing exists does not add anything to the description of that thing. An imaginary 100 gold coins has the same characteristics as 100 real gold coins. Existence is not itself an attribute or property, or as Russell would say, existence is not a predicate. In the proposition, 'Cows have udders', 'udders' is the predicate. The predicate 'udders' adds to a description of cows. To say, 'Cows exist', however, does not add anything to a description of cows. Rather, as John H. Hick argues:

> 'Cows exist' means 'There are *x*'s such that "*x* is a cow" is true.' This translation makes it clear that to say that cows exist is not to attribute a certain quality (namely existence) to cows, but is to assert that there are objects in the world to which the description summarized in the word 'cow' applies. (*Philosophy of Religion*, p. 19)

The advocates of the Ontological Argument cheat by slipping 'exists' in amongst the attributes of the idea of God. They try to make 'exists' not only an attribute or predicate of 'God' but a *necessary* predicate, when in fact it is not a predicate at all.

If God exists then his existence has to be established by means other than the Ontological Argument. It is not possible to prove God's existence, or the existence of anything else for that matter, by playing fast and lose with the rules of language and logic.

The refutations offered by Kant, Russell and others completely undermine the Ontological Argument. As said, the argument doesn't work. It is an argument that relies on logic that is clearly illogical. The consequences of the failure of the Ontological Argument for Descartes are serious. He fails to prove God's existence and without God he has nothing to guarantee that the external world exists. He not only fails to prove that the external world exists in exactly the way it appears to exist, he fails to prove that it exists at all. He slips right back to where he was at the end of the method of doubt, right back to 'I think therefore I am' with no certainty about anything beyond the existence of his own mind. As various critics have noted, Descartes' philosophy ultimately collapses into the solipsism it was designed to overcome once and for all.

When we began it seemed that the difficulty lay in finding reasons to doubt the existence of the external world. Now it appears it is far easier to raise doubts about its existence than to prove its existence. Science can't prove the external world exists because science relies on sensory evidence the reliability of which can always be questioned. It is possible that my sensations, my perceptions, never correspond to anything real, that the entire universe is simply a dream. And reason can't prove the external world exists because it is not possible to reason from the mere idea of a thing to the existence of that thing.

Descartes does not think that having the idea that there is an external world implies that there is an external world, but he does think that having the idea that there is a God implies that there is a God. So he tries to prove the existence of the external world that way, by making God the guarantor of the existence of the external world. But as we have seen, the idea of God does not imply the existence of God, so Descartes is denied his seemingly very clever, around-the-houses, *a priori* proof of the external world.

Dispelling these clouds

In the end it seems it is not possible to prove the existence of the external world. Scepticism regarding the external world demands a standard of proof so high that it simply can't be met. All the philosophical doubts raised in this chapter about the certainty of the external world remain. I was going to add, remain to haunt us, but why should they haunt us? Descartes was haunted by these doubts because he thought that he needed to prove the existence of the external world once and for all in order for science to proceed from a firm foundation. But he didn't prove the existence of the external world and science seems to have proceeded just fine on the basis of the *assumption* that the external world is real.

Actually, I'm not haunted by my doubts about the existence of the external world, or at least they only haunt me in a very artificial way when I'm doing philosophy. When I get out and about, I'm too busy interacting with the world that *appears* to be there to think about whether or not it is *really* there. The only time the thought sneaks up on me is when I'm in a particularly boring or unpleasant situation and I think, 'If this is all a virtual reality why can't I change the programme to my favourite restaurant or a paradise beach?' If I do not question the existence of the external world then I continually affirm it with my behaviour. Whatever philosophical doubts I can work up regarding the external world, I continue to act as though it exists. How could I act in any other way? What would it be to *act* as though one had doubts about the existence of the external world? My actions here are a case in point. I'm doubting the external world while at the same time *assuming* I am addressing readers, other minds, out there in the world. Recall Russell's point noted earlier that solipsism is psychologically impossible to believe.

In the end, if reason can't prove the existence of the external world then so much the worse for reason. Many philosophers argue that philosophy should give up trying to prove what can't be proven, what has certainly not been proven to this day, and get on with the job of analysing, describing and classifying perceptions as they appear to us. Never mind if there is or is not anything *beyond* appearances, we have the appearances and they are what philosophy should focus on and investigate.

The empiricist philosopher, David Hume, always an eminently sensible fellow, the canniest of canny Scots, thought very much along these lines. Indeed, he inspired a whole tradition of thinking along these lines. In true empiricist style he does not attempt to prove the existence of the external world because he thinks that to attempt such a proof is to attempt to go beyond the limits of our knowledge, beyond sensory experience, into the realms of futile metaphysical speculation. He concludes with true worldly wisdom that it is nature herself rather than metaphysical reasoning that dispels the most intractable and troubling philosophical doubts and problems. He writes:

> Most fortunately it happens, that since reason is incapable of dispelling these clouds, nature herself suffices to that purpose, and cures me of this philosophical melancholy and delirium, either by relaxing this bent of mind, or by some avocation, and lively impression of my senses, which obliterate all these chimeras. I dine, I play a game of back-gammon, I converse, and am merry with my friends; and when after three or four hours' amusement, I wou'd return to these speculations, they appear so cold, and strain'd, and ridiculous, that I cannot find in my heart to enter into them any farther. (*A Treatise of Human Nature*, p. 269)

3 How to be a Philosopher – Phase Two: The Tree Question

Family Guy in the forest

Some readers will be familiar with the cult of *Family Guy*. *Family Guy* is an American, adult cartoon show created by Seth MacFarlane featuring the crazy antics of the dysfunctional Griffin family and their neighbours. The show explores, sends-up and punctures every taboo, every political, social, personal and sexual issue that right-minded people think they must be sensitive, polite, respectful and sanctimonious about, raising political incorrectness to an art form in the process. *Family Guy* deliberately courts controversy by cruelly insulting everything and everyone – it is extremely impartial and non-discriminatory in that respect – and some of its more easily offended, reactionary critics believe it to be the devil incarnate. Others simply dismiss it as puerile, which it certainly is in many ways. It is a cartoon after all, with all the silly, immature, zany antics that one expects from the best cartoons. But to label it as puerile in order to dismiss it is to overlook its thoughtful and at times profoundly philosophical side . . . . This chapter is not meant to be a critique of a modern cultural phenomenon, an in depth analysis of the piss-taking prowess of MacFarlane and his team, so I'll cut to the chase.

In a classic episode called, The *Son Also Draws*, overweight family guy, Peter Griffin, and his overweight teenage son, Chris, are sent on a vision quest – a sacred spiritual journey into the wilderness without food, water or shoes – by a tribe of casino owning native Americans who have lost touch with their primitive roots. I once came across a whole web page dedicated to the condemnation of this episode and its allegedly racist misrepresentation of indigenous North American peoples, but enough of that.

Delirious with tiredness and the hunger of not having snacked for hours, Peter starts talking to a tree, or rather the tree starts talking to him. Quickly getting over the shock of communicating with nature, Peter seizes the opportunity to ask the tree a perennially popular philosophical question: 'Eh, tree. If one of you falls and there's no one around, do you make a noise?' Of course, if trees could talk then we would already have an answer to this question. They could tell us what happens when they fall or we could deduce that if they can talk they can hear and can therefore hear themselves fall. But as far as we know trees can't talk or hear and indeed are not conscious. They don't have any of the required apparatus for these functions. It is of course possible to go on debating whether or not plants have consciousness, and there are certainly people who believe that they do, but the focus of our debate here is somewhat different.

Away from the crazy world of cartoons, Peter's question is not normally put directly to trees themselves, although when I'm in the forest later today I'll give it a try. The question is normally framed like this: 'When a tree falls over in a forest and there is no one around, does it make a sound?' Actually, the question need not be about a tree. The tree as such is irrelevant. It could be a question about waves crashing on a deserted beach or a shelf collapsing in an empty room. The essence of the question is, 'Does sound still exist out of hearing?' Or even more fundamentally, 'What is the world like when it is not being experienced by anyone? Is it the same as when it is being experienced or is it radically different?'

As in the previous chapter, I want you to think about all this for yourself before I offer you the various answers that philosophers have formulated in the past. I want you to stop reading this book, sit back and do your own philosophizing about the famous question concerning the falling tree. Rather than just sit back, perhaps you'd like to go and discuss it with friends over coffee or something stronger or maybe even take a long, solitary walk in the forest to really get your philosophical thoughts together.

Before you commence contemplating, delving and deliberating I'll tell you what happens to Peter Griffin. The tree replies to his question in no uncertain terms: 'Are you kidding? Scot fell last week and he hasn't shut up about it since.' Snapped at the base, prostrate and understandably hysterical at his plight, Scot cries out, 'Sure, stand there and bitch, but would any of you take the time to help me?' Putting an end to all this nonsense Peter's spiritual guide appears in the form of a giant vision of The Fonz. . . .

How did it go? Did you discuss the tree question with friends or did you manage to scare them away the moment you opened your mouth and posed the question? Perhaps you took that long, solitary walk in the forest and tried putting the question to the trees themselves. Any luck? Anyway, here are some of the responses that have been made to the famous tree question. Some of them are responses made over the years by my philosophy students after just a few minutes of consideration, others are responses that result from a slightly more in depth analysis of the nature of reality and the nature of our relationship to it as creatures with sense organs and consciousness.

Ask a stupid question

The first response, what might positively be called the practical response, and negatively the dismissive response, is summed up in the expressions, 'Who cares?' and 'What a stupid question!' This is actually a perfectly sensible and intelligent response to the tree question, a question that, after all, has no real bearing on ordinary, everyday life and may in the end have no clear, final answer. But it is the very opposite of a philosophical response. I tell my philosophy students in the nicest possible way that if any of them feel compelled to answer with 'Who cares?' or 'What a stupid question!' then philosophy is probably not for them and they should consider switching to a different course.

I have a worksheet titled *That Tree Again!* which focuses on the tree question. I hand it out very early on in the philosophy course, during the induction period, in order to help students decide whether or not they have the right kind of intellectual curiosity that suits a person to the study of philosophy, the habit of questioning what is ordinarily not questioned. You may have come up with 'Who cares?' or 'What a stupid question!' as possible responses, but if they're your only responses then I'm amazed you've bothered to read this far into this book. Then again, you may have read this far into this book as a way of deciding once and for all what you've long suspected, that philosophy and philosophizing have little or nothing to do with the price of bread and are definitely not for you.

Common sense realism

Another somewhat less dismissive response to the tree question might be called the common sense response: A common sense person will exclaim, 'Of course the tree makes a sound!' It makes perfect sense to suppose that the world when it is not appearing to us is as it is when it is appearing to us and this, indeed, is how we imagine it. We would perhaps struggle to imagine it differently. If I close my eyes while sitting at this desk and try to conjure up a picture of the forest where I regularly walk and cycle, as it is right now at this precise moment, I imagine it just as it is when I'm there. The light through the branches, the leaves rustling in the breeze, boughs creaking, the crashing, splintering sound that any one of those trees would make right now if it fell over.

The view that the world appears to us exactly as it is in itself is known as direct, common sense or naïve realism. The direct realist view that a place when it is deserted is just as it is when someone is present is not only a perfectly sensible, common sense position to hold, it is, so to speak, the natural attitude to reality that we all have and perhaps need to have in our everyday lives. Ordinarily, we can't help assuming that the world when we are not there is as it is when we are there, undergoing its own motions and processes, brightening in the sunlight, dimming in the shade, releasing smells and making noises. In the fine words of the poet, Thomas Gray:

Full many a gem of purest ray serene,
The dark unfathomed caves of ocean bear;
Full many a flower is born to blush unseen,
And waste its sweetness on the desert air.

(*Elegy Written In A Country Churchyard*)

But for all the common sense of direct realism it is ultimately a position based on an assumption, and remember that as cold-blooded philosophers, rather than warm-blooded poets like Gray, we are in the ruthless Socratic business of destroying assumptions; the business of taking nothing for granted.

To claim that a place when it is deserted is just as it is when someone is present is to make a huge assumption for the simple reason that I can't *know* for sure what a place is like when I'm not there. I can, of course, place a camera and microphone there that send live pictures and sound to a TV in my study, but that in effect is only another way of being there – a technological way of extending the reach of at least some of my senses to the place in question. The tree question specifically asks what a place is like when there is *no* awareness of it. When I imagine the richness of the sights, sounds and smells of the deserted forest as it is right now as I sit typing in my study, I imagine myself there,

I recall what it is like at those times when I'm there and apply that image to this time, but the point is that I'm not there now at this time. For a person to claim to *know* that a falling tree makes a sound when there is no one around is for him to claim to know what it is like where he is not. But as it is logically impossible for a person to be where he is not he can't ever know for sure what it is like where he is not.

In a sense, the impossibility of proving or disproving that falling trees make a sound when there is no one around is the impossibility of being where one is not. In fact, what the falling tree question is really asking is, 'What is it like to be where there is no one?', which is surely a question that it is impossible to answer in any final, satisfactory way, except to say, 'I don't know'. Perhaps this is the conclusion you reached in your own deliberations on the tree question.

Philosophers have to be satisfied with the answer 'I don't know' far more often than many unphilosophically minded people think. I have to say that at least some of my philosophy students appear to believe that as their teacher I only pretend not to be in possession of all the answers; that I'm keeping them up my sleeve to be revealed with a fanfare at the end of the course. This is understandable as their experience of the world prior to studying philosophy is that teachers have the answers; that's why they're teachers.

Even if the absolute, final answer to the tree question has to be 'I don't know', there is still a lot of fascinating philosophical theorizing that has arisen in response to it and questions like it. I'll explore some of this theorizing shortly, but first, I want to consider the no nonsense response that a group of philosophers called logical positivists would make to the tree question and to questions like it.

The Vienna Circle and no nonsense logical positivism

In Vienna in 1923 a group of philosophers that included, amongst others, Rudolf Carnap, Herbert Feigl and Victor Kraft, started meeting at private Saturday morning seminars chaired by Moritz Schlick to forge a philosophy that has come to be known as logical positivism. The fact that they were prepared to meet on a Saturday to philosophize rather than go shopping or play five-a-side football shows just how keen they were. Actually, other sources say they met on a Thursday evening, but that hardly matters. What matters is that all or some of them constantly met at various venues in Vienna on various days of the week over a significant period of time.

Incidentally, the high concentration of world-class philosophers, psychologists, artists and musicians to be found knocking around Vienna during this period is truly amazing. I'll leave you to conduct your own researches and compile your own impressive list but undoubtedly, during the early part of the twentieth century, Vienna was the cultural capital of the world. Anyway, not surprisingly, the group of philosophers who met in Vienna from 1923 onwards came to be known as the Vienna Circle. They continued meeting on and off for many years until the gathering clouds of World War II forced most of them into exile.

The Vienna Circle had a huge influence on twentieth-century philosophy with many of the leading philosophers of the day attending their seminars at one time or another. The Viennese born Ludwig Wittgenstein, arguably the most important philosopher of the twentieth century, was a fringe member of the Circle. He refused to attend the full-blown meetings of the Circle because he did not subscribe entirely to their logical positivist views, but he met on his own terms with a carefully chosen selection of members – a kind of Vienna Inner Circle. According to Wittgenstein's biographer, Ray Monk, this select group had to be careful not to ask the highly strung Wittgenstein too many direct questions as these disturbed him greatly. 'Sometimes,' writes Monk, 'to the surprise of his audience, Wittgenstein would turn his back on them and read poetry' (*Ludwig Wittgenstein: The Duty of Genius*, p. 243). This was to show his contempt for their lack of appreciation of the *mystical* elements in his early philosophy as expressed in his great work, *Tractautus Logico-Philosophicus*, a book they greatly admired.

From 1930 to 1939 the Vienna Circle published a journal, *Erkenntnis* (meaning: knowledge recognition or cognition) which helped to spread the philosophy of logical positivism throughout Europe and the rest of the world. Interestingly, this journal was restarted in 1975 and is still going.

Logical positivism was imported into Britain largely by Sir Alfred Jules Ayer, much better known as A. J. Ayer (Freddie Ayer to his mates), who first became familiar with logical positivism during a postgraduate stay in Vienna in 1932. Ayer introduced himself to Schlick who not only invited the young man to his lectures but also gifted him the rare privilege of an invitation to the meetings of the Vienna Circle itself. Four years later in 1936, at the age of only 25, Ayer published the highly influential, *Language, Truth and Logic*, a work which has been hailed, not least by its publisher, as the classic manifesto of logical positivism.

The central aim of logical positivism was and is to clean up philosophy in order to render it compatible with the methods and principles of modern science. The logical positivists boldly argue that many if not most of the claims, statements and arguments put forward by philosophers throughout the long history of the subject are not true or false but in actual fact simply *meaningless*. That is to say, historically, most philosophers have spent their time asking questions and offering answers that have only a superficial veneer of grammatical sense beneath which there is only to be found nonsense and a deep confusion about the true nature and limits of language.

The logical positivists take their inspiration from the eighteenth-century empiricist philosopher, David Hume, whose great name has already cropped up repeatedly in this book. It is fair to say that the logical positivists revere Hume as the founding father and supreme head honcho of their school of thought. Understanding why the logical positivists are so influenced by Hume is probably the easiest way to understand exactly what logical positivism is and why it makes the radical claims it makes about philosophy.

David Hume and no nonsense logical positivism

As an empiricist Hume has no time for metaphysics. He totally rejects the view that knowledge of the world can be gained through pure abstract reasoning. He rejects, for example, the Ontological Argument, the metaphysical argument for the existence of God we looked at earlier, the argument that says the very idea of God implies the existence of God. As was mentioned way back in Chapter 1, he even dared to say that all books of metaphysics should be burnt as they 'contain nothing but sophistry and illusion' (*Enquiries*, p. 165). For Hume, the mind at birth is a blank slate, a *tabula rasa* as his empiricist predecessor John Locke called it, and all the knowledge that gets written on this slate must arrive through the senses, through *experience*. Hume argued that there are only two types of thing that it is possible for us to know – *relations of ideas* and *matters of fact*.

Relations of ideas refers to all the purely logical relationships that are found, for example, in maths and geometry. The mind has the capacity to recognize that the idea '2+2', for example, is equivalent to the idea '4'. On this basis the mind can immediately conclude that the statement or proposition '2+2=4' is absolutely certain. The same can be said for a geometrical proposition like, 'A triangle is a shape with three straight sides.' 'Triangle' just *means* 'shape with three straight sides' so there is no doubting the certainty of the proposition. The proposition, 'A father is a male parent' also expresses a relation of ideas. Once a person has learnt what the terms 'father' and 'male parent' mean, the truth of the proposition 'A father is a male parent' is unavoidable.

Hume's *relations of ideas* are today called *analytic propositions*. Such propositions simply exhibit logic rather than any kind of metaphysical knowledge. They do not really tell us anything about the world, and certainly nothing about worlds beyond the scope of the senses as metaphysics aims to do. They are self-referential, concerned only with themselves, so to speak. As Hume says, 'Propositions of this kind are discoverable by the mere operation of thought, without dependence on what is anywhere existent in the universe' (*Enquiries*, p. 25).

Matters of fact include all those propositions that are held to be true on the basis of the present evidence of our senses or the evidence of past experience as recorded by our memory. 'The grass is green', 'The sky is blue', 'London is the capital of England' and so on. Hume's *matters of fact* are today called *synthetic propositions*. Most of our talking and thinking is made up of synthetic propositions. If my wife asks me where the car keys are and I reply, 'The car keys are on the table' I have replied with a synthetic proposition. I have stated, as a *matter of fact*, on the basis of the evidence of my senses, that a given situation in the world is the case.

Unlike analytic propositions, synthetic propositions are not demonstrably certain as there is no contradiction involved in denying them. To deny that a father is a male parent is a contradiction, whereas it is not a contradiction to deny that the car keys are on the table. Even if the car keys are on the table, and they haven't been moved since I last saw them, it is possible to think of them as not being on the table, whereas it is not possible to think of a father as not being a male parent.

A synthetic proposition is only as certain as the evidence of the senses, and as we saw repeatedly in the last chapter, the senses are unreliable. The truth of the synthetic proposition, 'London is the capital of England' may seem pretty certain, but how do you know that London hasn't very recently ceased to be the capital of England? Perhaps, due to some political crisis, another English city has suddenly been designated the capital. To establish that this isn't so you would have to check with the usual news sources to see if London is still the capital of England, and providing you can trust these sources and your own senses you can be reasonably confident, but never absolutely certain, that London is the capital of England. It is possible only to have different degrees of *belief* in matters of fact, never *knowledge* in the strict sense of the word.

According to Hume, only propositions that express relations of ideas or matters of fact – only analytic and synthetic propositions – are *meaningful.* All other kinds of proposition, such as all the statements of metaphysics, for example, are meaningless. Any analytic proposition will be either a truism, what is technically called a *tautology*, with the logical form *x* is *x*, or a contradiction with the logical form *x* is not *x*. Any synthetic proposition will be either true or false depending on whether or not it correctly describes a situation in the empirical world. Any proposition that can't be shown to be a tautology or a contradiction, or empirically true or false, is simply *nonsense.*

Hume's division between relations of ideas and matters of fact has come to be known as *Hume's fork.* Unlike the table forks in my cutlery drawer which have four prongs, or the devil's trident which has three prongs, Hume's fork is definitely a two prong meat fork. If a proposition can't be impaled on either of its two prongs then it falls away into the scrap bin of nonsensical gobbledygook simply because there is just no way of ever establishing the truth or falsehood of what it is claiming.

Which type is the assertion of Hume's fork?

The verification principle

It is the two sharp, shiny prongs of Hume's fork that most fascinate the logical positivists. At the heart of their philosophy is something called the *verifiability principle* or *verification principle*. *Verification* is, according to the dictionary, the establishment of the correctness of a fact or theory. What the verification principle is has already been more or less explained via the explanation of Hume's fork given above. The short version of the principle is: 'All proposition are true, false or meaningless.' A longer formulation of the principle is: 'Propositions that cannot be verified as tautologies or contradictions on the basis of pure logic, or verified as true or false on the basis of empirical evidence, are unverifiable and therefore meaningless.'

Logical positivists recognize that there are many synthetic propositions the truth or falsehood of which has not yet been established. They allow that these propositions are meaningful if they are *verifiable in principle*. That is, if it is empirically, scientifically possible to establish their truth or falsehood even if nobody has yet managed to do so. Suppose I say, 'There is a wrecked sailing ship on the far side of Pluto.' My guess is that this synthetic proposition is false, but as nobody has yet conducted a very close examination of the far side of Pluto, the truth or falsehood of this proposition – what is technically called its *truth value* – has not yet been established. Its truth value is currently unverified, but it is not unverifiable as it is possible to say what evidence would verify it. It is, therefore, a meaningful proposition. Incidentally, as I write this, a NASA probe called New Horizons is hurtling towards Pluto at 36,000 mph and has been since 2006. When it gets there in the year 2015, it will gather the evidence that will verify the truth value of the proposition in question.

Wielding the verification principle the logical positivists aimed to tidy up philosophy, indeed, to tidy up all human reasoning. Logic and maths would remain on the one side or prong, and empirical science would remain on the other. All other thinking that was neither purely logical nor purely scientific, such as metaphysics, ethics and aesthetics, would be cast aside as nonsense. The most that these ancient areas of discourse could hope for in future was to be placed on a par with poetry; to be treated as collections of utterances, imperatives and exclamations expressing feelings, emotions, hopes and aspirations rather than as collections of meaningful propositions stating facts and falsehoods. Recall Ayer's radical claim noted in Chapter 1 that the moral statement, 'Stealing money is wrong,' has no factual meaning but simply expresses a 'special sort of moral disapproval' (*Language, Truth and Logic*, p. 110). As we would expect from the man who was largely responsible for importing logical positivism into Britain, this is a claim drawn from the very hub of the Vienna Circle.

Before finally getting back to that tree in the forest and saying how the logical positivists would respond to the tree question, I can't resist noting a major problem with logical positivism that the logical positivists tried hard to wriggle out of but never quite managed to escape.

The verification principle, it seems, is meaningless under its own terms. It expresses neither a logical relation of ideas – it is not a tautology or set of tautologies – nor an empirically verifiable matter of fact or fiction. Arguably, the person who accepts the principle as true is committed, by the principle, to dismissing it as nonsense! Ouch!

You have probably already guessed what the logical positivists would say in response to the tree question. Any answer that was given to the question, other than an entirely neutral, noncommittal answer such as, 'I don't know', would be entirely meaningless and nonsensical. In other words, the tree question does not and cannot have a meaningful answer and as such is not a genuine question.

Basically, only two answers, two propositions, can be given in response to the tree question: 'A falling tree makes a sound when nobody is around to hear it.' 'A falling tree does not make a sound when nobody is around to hear it.' Both these answers are equally unverifiable as true or false. They are not answers that rely on logic and neither are they answers that can be judged in the light of empirical evidence. By asking, in essence, 'What is the world like when there is no creature with sense organs present?', the very question which invites these answers *prohibits* the use of empirical evidence. Therefore, both these answers, or so-called answers, are equally devoid of meaning. The logical positivists would argue that along with the question, these answers belong to the realm of empty, vacuous, barren metaphysical speculation.

Sound is consciousness of sound

So far we've considered common sense arguments to the effect that the falling tree in question makes a sound, and stronger logical positivist arguments to the effect that any answer to the tree question except 'I don't know' is bound to be meaningless. Even if the absolute, final, safe answer to the tree question has to be 'I don't know', there is nonetheless a lot of intriguing philosophical theorizing that has arisen in response to it and questions like it that tends towards the conclusion that things do not and cannot make a sound in the absence of consciousness.

There is a question that is perhaps long overdue in the asking: What is sound? The first definition of the word 'sound' offered by my faithful dictionary is: 'a periodic disturbance in the pressure or density of a fluid or in the elastic strain of a solid, produced by a vibrating object. It travels in longitudinal waves'. In short, sound is vibrations in stuff. This, of course, is not the whole picture, which is why the second definition offered by my dictionary is: 'the sensation produced by such a periodic disturbance in the organs of hearing'. Vibration, such as the vibration made by a tree when it falls over, is a necessary condition of sound, but it is not a sufficient condition. Vibration alone is not sound. There must not only be a functioning ear or two to sense the vibration but also a mind to be conscious of the sensation.

We sometimes say of a person who is unconscious, even if his ears are functioning perfectly, 'He can't hear anything.' Sound, as distinct from vibrations in the air and activity in the ears and auditory nerve, is first and foremost consciousness of sound, but for there to be consciousness of sound, consciousness must be one of an ensemble of elements that also includes vibrations and functioning ears.

This line of reasoning leads to the conclusion that the tree that falls over in a forest when there is no one around does not make a sound. There may be vibrations in the tree, in the ground, in the air all around, but if there is no conscious creature present with the right kind of functioning sense organs to be aware of these vibrations in the form of sound then there is no sound. There is also no sound if there is a living creature present but it is in such a deep coma that it has no awareness of its surroundings. Similarly, there is no sound if there is a conscious creature present but it is profoundly deaf, either because its ears don't function or because it never had any ears in the first place. There is some sense in saying that the world of the profoundly deaf person is full of sounds that he can't hear, but what is really being said is that the world the profoundly deaf person inhabits is full of sounds for other people who can hear. The world of the profoundly deaf person contains no sound, otherwise he would not be deaf.

Claiming that a falling tree makes no sound unless there is a conscious creature present to the vibrations the falling tree produces that is capable of being aware of these vibrations as sound, raises far more general questions regarding the nature of the world in the absence of consciousness. As was noted at the start of this chapter, the tree as such is irrelevant. The essence of the tree question is not so much, 'Does sound still exist out of hearing?', as, 'What is the world like when it is not being experienced by any one? Is it the same as when it is being experienced or is it radically different?' One branch of philosophy that addresses this question goes by the fancy title of transcendental idealism.

Kant and transcendental idealism

Transcendental idealism is primarily the philosophy of its founder, the great eighteenth-century German philosopher, Immanual Kant, whose illustrious name has already been mentioned repeatedly in this book. Kant is a true giant of philosophy who is referred to and deferred to endlessly by other philosophers. If great philosophers are mountains, then Kant is definitely one of the higher peaks of the Himalayas. The shadow he casts is enormous. His influence is such that many philosophers to this day still describe themselves as post-Kantians. In *Zen and the Art of Motorcycle Maintenance*, Robert M. Pirsig describes Kant as having a mind like a laser beam capable of zeroing in on the heart of a philosophical problem. Pirsig says: 'Kant is always superbly methodical, persistent, regular and meticulous as he scales that great snowy mountain of thought concerning what is inside the mind and what is outside the mind. It is, for modern climbers, one of the highest peaks of all . . .' (*Zen and the Art of Motorcycle Maintenance*, p. 133).

Kant was most famous for 3 things: (1) for never travelling more than 10 miles from his home town of Königsberg in German East Prussia (now a German speaking exclave of Russia wedged between Lithuania and Poland); (2) for taking a walk at exactly the same time every afternoon except on the day when he received a copy of David Hume's *Treatise* and became too engrossed in it to go out; and (3) for writing a series of major critiques that redefined philosophy. The first and most important of these critiques is the *Critique of Pure Reason* (1781), the work in which Kant sets out his philosophy of transcendental idealism.

Kant was influenced both by the rationalist, metaphysical thinking of Descartes and Leibniz and by the new ideas of their opponents, the British empiricists, Locke and Hume. In the Preface of his *Prolegomena to Any Future Metaphysics*, Kant praises Hume for interrupting his 'dogmatic slumber' (*Prolegomena*, p. 5), although he does not mention the legendary missed walk. From the moment he discovered Hume, Kant began to reconcile the two great philosophical traditions of rationalism and empiricism. Transcendental idealism is the result of that synthesis.

Kant considers the empiricist view of Locke and Hume that everything we know comes to us through our senses. He also considers the rationalist view of Plato, Descartes and Leibniz that true knowledge is achieved through pure *a priori* reasoning without the senses. He decides that both these views have value but that each only tells half the story. Kant agrees with the empiricists that we can't know anything without our senses. If we did not receive sensory impressions of the outside world our minds would be empty and blank. However, he disagrees with the empiricists that sensory impressions *alone* are enough to give us knowledge of the world. Our sensory impressions of the world would remain confused, disorganized and meaningless if the mind did not have the capacity to organize them. Kant argues that the mind *organizes* the raw sensory data that it receives from the world into meaningful experience. In a sense, the mind is nothing but this capacity to organize the raw sensory data that it gets from the world.

Kant sometimes calls the raw, empirical, sensory data that comes from the world *percepts*. The mind, he argues, imposes *a priori concepts* on the percepts in order to organize them and produce intelligible, coherent experience of the world. For Kant then, experience of the world is a *synthesis* of percepts and concepts. The percepts are empirical, the concepts pure *a priori* rational principles. Kant said, 'Thoughts without content are empty, intuitions without concepts are blind' (*Critique of Pure Reason*, p. 93). The widely accepted shorthand version of this maxim (or simplified translation from the German) is, 'Concepts without percepts are empty, percepts without concepts are blind.' The point is that concepts must have percepts to apply to or act upon in order to be more than mere empty abstractions; percepts must be acted upon by concepts in order to be illuminated, made sensible, organized and so on. In short, the mind organizes percepts through the application of concepts.

According to Kant, the two main concepts that order percepts are space and time. He argues that we do not derive our concepts of space and time from our experience of objects because it is not possible to have an experience of objects unless we think or conceive of them as existing in space and time. Our experience of the world presupposes space and time, it does not give us any impressions of space and time as things existing independently of objects. In short, we do not experience space and time as such, we experience *in terms of* space and time. They are not *what* we experience, they are the *way* we experience. Similarly, we do not experience such concepts as number or causation. These concepts are, instead, our means of organizing the world into something that is comprehensible to us.

This is not easy stuff to get your head around and you may need to reread it a few times or stop and reflect awhile in order to grasp the gist of it. Believe it or not, what I've given you here is a *simplified* version of Kant's theory! If you are grasping it loud and clear then well done, you're a natural. If it is currently passing a few inches over your head because you are hungry, tired, distracted or simply because you got

wasted last night then don't worry. What will almost certainly make
things clearer is thinking about the *implications* of Kant's theory.

The main implication of Kant's theory is that a clear distinction must
be drawn between the world as we experience it and the world as it is
in itself apart from our experience of it. Kant certainly draws this distinction, referring to the world as we experience it as the *world of
phenomena* and the world as it is in itself as the *world of noumena*.
The noumenal world is not spatial, temporal or characterised by causation, motion and so on, or at least, we can never know that it is. The
mind continually and unavoidably imposes time, space etc., on the
noumenal world, or whatever it is the mind receives from it, to the
extent that the world we are aware of, the phenomenal world, is
always a *representation*; an interpretation organized according to certain conceptual schemas.

The noumenal world is forever obscured by this representation. We
can never get at it. The phenomenal world appears to us, the noumenal world does not appear to us. We can know nothing of the noumenal world, except to say, perhaps, that it *is*. It is forever beyond our
experience, it transcends our experience. The world of phenomena we
experience is, Kant says, *phenomenally real*, even though it is, in a
sense, an appearance. The world of noumena is, Kant says, *transcend-
entally ideal*, even though it is, in a sense, what is truly real, what is
truly mind-independent.

'Real' becomes an incredibly slippery term in the hands of philosophers. Indeed, one measure of a person's progress in philosophy is
the increasing perplexity with which he regards the terms 'real' and
'reality'.

In making a distinction between noumena and phenomena is Kant
referring to two separate worlds or realities, or to two aspects of one
world or reality? That is, does Kant have a two worlds view or a two
aspects view? The two worlds view is perhaps a rather unsophisticated
view of Kant's distinction and most philosophers these days favour the
two aspects view, arguing that for Kant there is only a single reality

that can be encountered from two distinct standpoints. Only a divine mind capable of non-sensible intuition can encounter the world as noumena, as it is in itself. Ordinary minds capable only of sensible intuition must encounter the world as phenomena, as divided into distinct objects existing in space and time.

Arguably, Kant's theory suggests not only that falling trees do not make a sound in the absence of consciousness, but that there are no trees or any other distinct objects in the absence of consciousness. In arguing that the spatial, temporal, cause and effect world in motion that we inhabit is a *synthesis* of consciousness and whatever exists independently of consciousness, Kant's theory strongly suggest that the world as it is in itself apart from consciousness is what some post-Kantian philosophers refer to as *undifferentiated being*.

Sartre on differentiated and undifferentiated being

A philosopher who is not always recognized as being a post-Kantian but certainly is in many ways is the French existentialist, Jean-Paul Sartre. For Sartre, what there is, fundamentally, is being and non-being (nothingness). Sartre's notion of being, or what he calls being-in-itself, is very similar to Kant's notion of noumena. Being-in-itself *is* and that really is all that can be said of it. It is tempting to say that it has always been and always will be but that would imply that it has the characteristic of existing in time when it has no characteristics whatsoever other than existing. It is even more bland than an *X Factor* finalist and like him or her has no reason for existing. Sartre says:

> Being is superfluous . . . consciousness absolutely can not derive being from anything, either from another being or from a possibility, or from a necessary law. Uncreated, without reason for being, without any connection with another being, being-in-itself is *de trop* for eternity. (*Being and Nothingness*, p. 22)

Sartre also calls being-in-itself *undifferentiated being* as a way of stressing that it is devoid of contrasts, divisions, differences. No part of it is any different from any other part of it, which is to say, it does not have parts.

For Sartre, the only other kind of being is non-being or nothingness. Non-being is not really separate from being-in-itself, it exists only as a *relation* to being-in-itself. Strange to say, but it exists as the *denial* of being-in-itself, as a *lack* of being-in-itself, as the *negation* of being-in-itself and so on. Like a reflection in a mirror it borrows all of its being from what it reflects and sometimes Sartre even refers to it as a *borrowed being*. All this is heady stuff and to really grasp the mechanics of the relationship between being-in-itself and non-being you would have to read at least some of Sartre's vast treatise, *Being and Nothingness*, or one of the many commentaries on it.

The key point to grasp is that non-being or nothingness, or what Sartre usually refers to as *being-for-itself*, is consciousness, or at least the logical basis of consciousness. It is only when consciousness, which exists as nothing but a relationship to being-in-itself, applies itself to being-in-itself and begins carving it up and differentiating it into distinct phenomena – this as distinct from that, this as not that, this as external to that and so on – that the world of everyday phenomena arises, at least from our point of view. Not surprisingly – and you may have already guessed this – Sartre refers to the world of phenomena that appears to us as *differentiated being*. Sartre's distinction between differentiated and undifferentiated being is clearly very similar to Kant's two aspects view of reality.

There are times in his writings when Sartre talks like a direct realist, but the more deeply rooted tendency in his philosophy is towards transcendental idealism. For Sartre, the forest when there is no one there (if we can still call it a forest) is undifferentiated being. There is being-in-itself but there are no trees *as such* to fall, let alone make a sound. If a person finds the proverbial tree in the forest has fallen, as people often do, he does not know it fell. All he knows is that it is now lying where it once stood. Perhaps objects that move in our absence – supposing there are objects in our absence – do so by quantum leaps.

We seem to have philosophized ourselves into a very strange position indeed, and for the sake of our sanity we feel we need to ask if the world, apart from our consciousness of it, can really be so completely undifferentiated? Surely, the world has its own processes, patterns and motions quite apart from us. Surely, natural phenomena, such as plants and animals, have their own patterns of existence that do not require our interest in order to occur. Granted, the world we encounter is characterised in all sorts of ways by us. There is a definite sense in which the world is our world. To argue, however, that without the involvement of consciousness there is simply no world of phenomena at all seems to be an extremely self-centred view that disregards the evidence of nature.

Inconclusive conclusions

What is the way forward? Is there one? Perhaps the English empiricist John Locke can help us. Locke makes a very useful distinction between the primary and secondary qualities or properties of objects. Primary qualities of extension, figure, solidity, number and motion belong to objects themselves independently of us. Secondary qualities of colour, taste, smell and sound are in us, or more precisely in our relationship with the object. Secondary qualities belong to our perception of the object rather than the object itself.

There is something about the atomic structure of a ripe banana that makes me see it as yellow in ordinary light, but it is not yellow in itself. It is not yellow in the absence of light or when no one is perceiving it. Similarly, there is something about the atomic structure of a tree that makes me hear it make a certain crashing, splintering sound when it falls over, but a falling tree does not emit this sound as such when there is no one perceiving it. Recall what was said about sound requiring the ensemble of vibrations, ears and consciousness. Anyway, Locke's distinction between primary and secondary qualities appears to allow us to hold onto the common sense view that there are distinct objects in our absence, while accepting that objects do not have colours, tastes, smells or sounds until consciousness arrives on the scene.

The big problem with this seemingly neat Lockean 'get out of jail free card' lies in something Kant said. Namely, that to experience the world as a world of distinct objects, as a world of discrete phenomena, requires the application of the concepts of space and time. To claim that there are objects in the absence of consciousness, even objects with only primary qualities, is to claim, against Kant, that time and space exist in the absence of consciousness and are features of the world as it is in itself. Recall that, for Kant, time and space are concepts or schemas that the mind employs to organize the world into something intelligible.

Perhaps the neatest way out of these dire straits (I'll spare you any cheesy jokes about a certain 1980s smooth rock band) is to endorse the *idealism* of Bishop George Berkeley that we considered in Chapter 2. Recall Berkeley's argument that there is no material world, only collections of ideas perceived by the mind. Locke's distinction between primary and secondary qualities no longer really holds for Berkeley, every quality is just a different kind of idea in the mind. A tree is one set of ideas, the sounds the tree makes as it falls over another. 'To be is to be perceived,' said Berkeley, meaning that all ideas exist only in so far as they are perceived by a mind. For Berkeley, there is no longer any problem of deciding what belongs to the mind and what belongs to the world in itself because his theory insists that everything belongs to the mind.

Berkeley is no fool and he recognizes that his theory needs a magic ingredient if it is not to be indistinguishable from solipsism. He argues that the world, as a collection of ideas, exists independently of me when I'm not perceiving it because an omniscient, omnipresent, omnipotent God perceives all of it all of the time. Recall Knox's excellent limerick in which God says that the tree continues to be when there is no one about in the Quad because he, God, perceives it. Berkeley himself says:

> All those bodies which compose the mighty frame of the world, have not any subsistence without a mind, that their being is to be perceived or known; that consequently so long as they are not actually perceived by me, or do not exist in my mind or that of any other created spirit, they must either have no existence at all, or else subsist in the mind of some eternal spirit. (*Principles of Human Knowledge*, p. 55)

So, Berkeley's answer to the tree question would be unequivocal. The tree exists – as a collection of ideas – and it makes a noise as it falls because God hears it. Simple. It is a beautiful solution to all the problems that have perplexed and tortured us in this chapter. There is only one tiny loose end to tie up before we can give it our unqualified, wholehearted consent – we must prove the existence of God!

4 How to Make a Living from Philosophy

By way of conclusion and as a means of bringing us all back down to reality – whatever reality is – I thought I'd take a not too serious but nonetheless honest look at the whole thorny issue of earning a crust from philosophy. After all, if you've found that this book has really whetted your appetite for philosophy, that you'd like to learn more about the subject, that you might even like to study it formally and gain qualifications in it – perhaps that is precisely what you are doing at the moment anyway – then it would be great if you could go on to make a living out of it. There is nothing in life better than being paid to do what you enjoy, well, not much anyway.

There is a surprisingly large amount of careers information available relating to philosophy, too much of it, perhaps, aimed at reassuring parents, who want their darling offspring to succeed where they failed, that studying Philosophy at college and university is not a one-way ticket to poverty and ruin. The most common form of reassurance given is that a Philosophy degree is an excellent passport to careers more or less unrelated to philosophy. As if to say, there is still hope for a young person's future success, and his or her parent's middle-class ambitions-by-proxy, even if he or she has studied philosophy.

A few Philosophy graduates do, of course, end up ruined in various ways. Some succumb to nihilism and despair of *Schopenhauerian* proportions, while others discover the kind of self-abusive spirituality that inspires a person to give away his inheritance and start begging on the streets of Calcutta. A handful even discover that a Philosophy degree is a passport to the utter spiritual ruin and moral degradation of a career in banking. In all cases, personal choice and factors totally unrelated to philosophy make the decisive contribution to the downfall.

Now, it is certainly true that a Philosophy degree is an excellent passport to all sorts of careers. As I said in my introduction to this book, studying philosophy gives a person the ultimate transferable skill set. Trained philosophers learn quickly and deeply because they understand the basic principles of all knowledge. Their ability to question, analyse, explore and conceptualize in ways that would not occur to non-philosophers makes them excellent problem solvers and innovators. They have the capacity to reason, write and speak coherently which makes them a valuable asset to many of the best employers. Research has repeatedly shown that Philosophy graduates come a close second to specialists on a whole range of post degree vocational courses.

Research has also shown that Philosophy graduates, being discerning creatures, tend to take longer to find their career path after graduating. However, when they do find it, they often join the ranks of the most successful and inspired people in society. As the British Philosophical Association says on its web page titled, 'Careers for Philosophy Graduates':

> It is true that 'first destination' figures, which are collected three months after graduation, often show philosophy graduates towards the bottom of the table. However, one reason for this is that many philosophy graduates have rejected the idea of a conventional path through life, and so seek more unusual forms of work, and so take their time to find the right opportunity.

The same web page also provides a list of high flying movers and shakers who gained a degree or two in Philosophy before going on to achieve great things in the world beyond philosophy's so-called ivory tower. The list includes children's TV presenter, Liz Barker; broadcaster and author, Jonathan Dimbleby; leading criminal defence lawyer, Michael Mansfield QC; Curator of Public Events at Tate Modern, Dominic Willsdon; comedian, writer and actor, Ricky Gervais and psychoanalyst and former England cricket captain, Mike Brearley OBE. I'm sure other countries could produce equally impressive lists of their successful Philosophy graduates but I'll leave you to conduct that research for yourself if you are so inclined.

In offering the paragraphs above I have slid into the familiar trap of feeling obliged to reassure people that qualifications in philosophy are useful *outside* the field of philosophy. Well, hopefully, now that I have fulfilled that obligation, or at least paid sufficient lip-service to it, I can get back to considering professional opportunities *within* the field of philosophy and how one goes about becoming a professional philosopher.

At this point, as a trained philosopher, I suddenly find myself obliged to ask what it is I *mean* by 'the field of philosophy'. Well, what is generally meant by this expression is all those people around the world who teach philosophy to students at various academic levels, conduct research into philosophy, attend conferences and seminars on philosophy, write books, papers, articles, columns, reviews and blogs about philosophy, or even occasionally feature on radio and television offering profound philosophical insights into everything from the crisis of capitalism to the cuteness of kittens.

Now, although this field does not employ anywhere near as many people as farming, retail or even hairdressing, it nevertheless employs several thousand people around the world, mainly in universities and colleges. It is, therefore, a legitimate goal to want to be a professional philosopher and it is likely that any young person with sufficient ability, drive, determination and patience will eventually become a professional philosopher if he or she genuinely and realistically chooses that goal.

I say young person because it can take years to become a professional philosopher – just as it takes years to become a lawyer or medical doctor. A significantly older person might not feel they have the years remaining to them, with their health and mental faculties intact, to scale what is a many-runged ladder. Certainly, an older person is less likely to be able or willing to tolerate being relatively hard-up while they become sufficiently qualified. While studying for my PhD in Philosophy I lived in a one bedroom garret where every winter the internal walls ran with condensation. I'm too old and spoilt by my bourgeois comforts to tolerate that now but back then I was so absorbed in the intricacies of Sartre's conception of consciousness, freedom and bad faith that the only thing I demanded from my surroundings was peace and quiet.

How one lives and how well one lives while studying philosophy obviously depends on how well-off one is. It certainly helps to have an understanding family, usually parents, who are able to contribute to at least some of your upkeep, but I don't think it is true, as some people claim, that philosophy is the preserve of the wealthy, although several of the great philosophers certainly came from highly privileged backgrounds.

Plato was an aristocrat who, like all ancient Greek aristocrats, had slaves. Bertrand Russell inherited the title of Earl and Wittgenstein was a member of one of Austria's wealthiest families. Generous to a fault and as naïve about the value of hard cash as only those born with a silver spoon in their mouth can be, Wittgenstein gave all of his money away. Fortunately, his considerable philosophical talents allowed him to earn a crust at Cambridge when the inheritance was gone.

Kant, on the other hand, was the son of a hard-working saddler, while Sartre was the son of a navel officer who died young and the grandson of a man who owned a language school and a large library. Most philosophers I know came from supportive but not particularly privileged backgrounds and they worked hard and pinched the pennies to get where they are today, or so they tell me. I myself was raised in a large family on a council estate where money was often tight. Before this vulgar display of my working class credentials inspires you to start playing the world's smallest violin, I'll quickly move on and say: It ain't where you're from but where you're at, or at least, where you're trying to get to.

How you fund yourself while you are becoming sufficiently qualified to become a professional philosopher is a problem for you, your family and the politicians who decide how much educational funding there is available. There is funding available for the study of philosophy – various grants and bursaries – but none of them is a king's ransom and beyond undergraduate level the competition for what there is is fierce. In the unlikely event that you fit the obscure applications criteria of a particular funding body – only three legged, vertically challenged, Gaelic, vampires need apply – the several forever lost days you will spend filling out lengthy, tedious, irritating and unfriendly forms are most likely to result months later in rejection at the hands of a commit-tee of high-handed dons who have unaccountably decided that the other guy's research proposal is more worthwhile than yours, even though you would have completed and he will spend the few hundred quid he receives on a skiing holiday. Still, if you can stand the bureau-cracy it's worth a try. Like any lottery, you've got to be in it to win it and it could be you.

So, unless you are rich, it is difficult but certainly not impossible in funding terms to get yourself sufficiently qualified in philosophy at postgraduate level. What can I say, the higher the fewer, but where there's a will there's a way and who dares wins and he or she who wills the end wills the means. Fortunately, many university Philosophy departments employ postgraduates as teaching assistants, helping them to gain teaching experience and make modest ends meet while they are studying.

One thing that has already become abundantly clear is that to become a professional philosopher you are almost certainly going to need very good qualifications. These days it is highly unlikely that any university in the world would take you on in a full-blown philosophy lecturing capacity without a PhD – a doctorate in Philosophy. To get a

PhD you have to write an 80,000 word thesis (approximately twice the length of the book you are reading now) on a philosophical topic of your own choosing that reflects extensive research and a level of originality. This thesis has to be approved by two professors of philosophy, one from your own university, the other from an external university.

These two professors have the power to reject several years' work as never going to be worthy of a PhD, although a student who has been correctly supervised should not be allowed to get to this stage. If a student is lucky, the two professors will wipe the floor with his work for a couple of hours in what is called a *viva voce* (oral examination) before referring his thesis back to him for extensive revision. This is called a referral. My thesis was referred, as many are. Before the professors would grant me the qualification, they sent me away to rewrite the first part, which basically involved ditching and replacing about 30,000 words. I was temporarily devastated, I'd hoped to emerge from the *viva* as a doctor, free to get on with the rest of my life, yet my supervisor phoned to congratulate me. In being referred I'd won through to the next stage rather than suffering outright rejection.

To be allowed to do a Philosophy PhD in the first place you have to have a good first degree such as a BA (Bachelor of Arts), or even a second degree such as an MA (Master of Arts). Well, nowhere have I said that becoming a professional philosopher was easy.

One slightly less arduous route, at least in qualification terms, is to aspire to teach philosophy at college level, what in Britain is called A-level and in the United States AP-level. To do this you would need a reasonably good BA in Philosophy and probably also a teaching qualification such as a PGCE (Postgraduate Certificate of Education). Teaching A-level or equivalent can be very rewarding if you prefer teaching philosophy to having to do research in it, although there is no doubt that it can be very challenging explaining even the basics of philosophy to teenagers with limited vocabularies who have generally never come across anything like it before and who often have strange and unhelpful preconceptions about what it involves.

The worst preconception is that Philosophy A-level or equivalent just involves sitting around talking about whatever comes up. Certainly, debate is a very important part of the study of philosophy, but all philosophy courses leading to formal qualifications are highly structured and require students to learn a significant amount of content relating to methods and procedures in philosophy, key philosophical texts, schools of thought and the history of ideas generally.

Unfortunately, the persistence of the preconception that philosophy just involves sitting around shooting the breeze means that college level Philosophy courses always attract a few of the least able and least motivated students – students looking for an easy time. They soon discover that philosophy is not a soft option, that more than any other subject on the curriculum it demands brains with more than one forward gear and an extraordinary level of intellectual tenacity. Successful philosophy students have to be able to think for themselves. Fortunately, Philosophy courses also invariably attract the brightest, most highly self-motivated, naturally curious and constructively argumentative students.

Increasingly, philosophy is taught in schools to pre-college level students. In Britain there are GCSEs in Philosophy and Ethics and Philosophy and Religious Studies, and many other countries have their equivalents. As at college, you would need a degree and a teaching qualification (or a teaching degree) to get into this line of work, although interestingly your degree need not necessarily be in philosophy. In most schools, philosophy is taught within the Religious Studies Department only to older, more able students, so the opportunity to teach philosophy in a school would almost certainly mean that you had to teach other stuff besides. Such subjects as Personal and Social Education, Citizenship and the happy-clappy, multicultural, uncritical take on the major world religions that constitutes the core of Religious Studies as taught to children.

Personal and Social Education (PSE), Citizenship and Religious Studies are all worthwhile subjects that contain or can be made to contain philosophical elements, but becoming a school Religious Studies teacher in order to teach philosophy is like becoming a soldier in order to travel.

The peculiar challenges of school teaching, the most personally demanding and potentially demoralizing of them being behaviour management, mean that a person would have to want to work with children first and foremost and want to be a philosopher a very distant second. None of this is to say that quite young children can't be taught philosophy at a reasonably sophisticated level, but they have to be ready and willing to learn.

Many philosophers make some money from writing philosophy books – a nice little supplement to their income – but very few if any earn their entire living from writing philosophy. The philosophy book market as a whole is huge, but the market for any one philosophy book is limited. A philosophy book that took years of painstaking work to complete just can't compete for sales with the average trashy celebrity biography tossed off by some ghost writer in a couple of weeks. And as the profit margins on any one philosophy book are limited, academic publishers can only offer the philosopher-author a small percentage of their net receipts – at least, that's what academic publishers always tell us!

The last few decades have seen the rise of the so-called pop philosopher, a trend perhaps started by Bertrand Russell and what he called his 'shilling shockers', books like *Why I am Not a Christian* and *In Praise of Idleness*. The pop philosopher writes philosophy in an entertaining, ordinary language style with the aim of making it accessible and relevant to a far wider audience than the formal, highly technical variety. With some clever marketing and the occasional accompanying TV or radio programme, the pop philosopher becomes a bit of a celebrity and his or her books climb to astronomical heights on Amazon's sales rank, only a few thousand places below *Yet Another Cookery Book* or Dan Brown's latest pseudo-intellectual thriller. Among today's most successful pop philosophers are Alain de Botton, Julian Baggini and A. C. Grayling.

Even pop philosophers, however, tend not to be able to live by book sales alone. They give talks, edit magazines and have lucrative part-time visiting lectureships tucked away at obscure universities like Oxford, Cambridge, Yale and Harvard. I won't deny that with this and my last book, *How to Be an Existentialist*, I'm aspiring to join the not entirely revered ranks of the pop philosopher but I would not presume to think that I had made it yet or ever will. I'm still waiting for that phone call from BBC Four, the one regarding flying me to Paris to make a hard-hitting documentary about the life and loves of Jean-Paul Sartre and Simone de Beauvoir.

Now, Sartre was one philosopher who certainly made a living out of writing philosophy to the extent that he no longer taught the subject except when he felt like it. But then Sartre is one of the most prolific writers in the history of writing, let alone the history of philosophy. For several decades he churned out vast theoretical works, articles, short stories, novels, plays, biographies and film scripts – all essentially philosophical in character – to the extent that he gained the nickname of 'the engine room'. He not only supported himself from his writings but an entourage of hangers-on as well. I'm not sure if Sartre was a millionaire. Being a true philosopher he did not care for material possessions so it is not possible to gauge his wealth from an inventory of what he owned. All we know is that he lived much of his life in Parisian hotel rooms, something that certainly wouldn't come cheap these days, and always had pockets full of cash to pick up the tab for all those rich French meals he enjoyed with his friends and hangers-on.

The following anecdote may well be apocryphal but I was once told by my own Logic lecturer that the logician, Irving M. Copi, was a philosophy millionaire with his own ocean going yacht. Copi, who died in 2002, is the author of an *Introduction to Logic*, a standard text on Logic courses throughout the world, currently into its thirteenth edition and retailing at an impressive $81.75. Copi is also the author of a top-selling study guide to his own introduction. I can't confirm the yacht but it is certainly true that Copi taught at the University of Hawaii at Manoa for 21 years from 1969–90. Nice work if you can get it. Who said it doesn't pay to be too logical?

So, it is difficult but not impossible to become a professional philosopher or even a philosophy millionaire. You just have to study hard, get to university, get a degree or three, preferably a PhD, publish several papers in respected philosophical journals or at least one book and beat the competition to a teaching post. A long, hard road for sure, but thousands of people have done it over the years and new people will continue to do it in future. Old professors of philosophy fall off their perches everyday and have to be replaced.

To be precise, you don't have to achieve all that before you can start earning a living from philosophy. There is the increasingly popular college route I mentioned where you don't need a PhD or publications to teach philosophy to pre-university students. Alternatively, you can at least start making a modest living from philosophy as soon as you get your first degree and become a postgraduate teaching assistant or fully funded research student.

I made a modest living from philosophy even as a PhD student. I was a part-time postgraduate teaching assistant, a part-time teacher of a couple of philosophy evening classes and a part-time private philosophy tutor. During one pre-exam period I had up to half a dozen philosophy students scattered around Birmingham, England. I visited them by bicycle one at a time, all on the same day, on what I called my 'philosophy round'. I delivered knowledge of Plato and Mill door to door for hard cash where others delivered milk and newspapers. These are the kind of lengths you may have to go to if you want to become a professional philosopher, so, on yer bike, as the saying goes.

Interestingly, it may well be possible to be a professional philosopher without being in the field of philosophy as I have defined it so far in this chapter. There are, as the pop philosopher Julian Baggini points out, plenty of people making a living out of philosophizing who would not describe themselves as philosophers. As Baggini writes: 'In the UK, for example, it is often thought philosophy is not an important part of the culture, but it's actually all over the place: in serious journalism, the work of think tanks, and in ethics committees. It's just not usually called "philosophy" ' ('A Class Apart', *The Guardian*, 2008).

So, arguably, you can become a professional philosopher simply by getting your foot in the door of one of the many careers outside of academic philosophy where philosophizing plays a significant role – novelist, poet, playwright, film director, priest, stand up comedian, existential counsellor, taxi driver, gravedigger. Perhaps all you need to do is sit on a street corner in white robes with a begging bowl engaging passers-by in more than superficial conversation, but be careful who you upset.

Bibliography

Allen, Woody, *Side Effects* (New York: Ballantine, 1991).

Anselm, *Proslogion*, trans. M. J. Charlesworth (Oxford: Clarendon, 1965).

Aristotle, *The Nicomachean Ethics*, trans. J. A. K. Thomson (London: Penguin, 2004).

Ayer, A. J., *Language, Truth and Logic* (London: Penguin: 2001).

Ayer, A. J., *The Problem of Knowledge* (London: Penguin, 1990).

Baggini, Julian, 'A Class Apart', *The Guardian*, 30 July, 2008.

Berkeley, George, *Principles of Human Knowledge* (London: Penguin, 2005).

Blackburn, Simon, *Being Good: A Short introduction to Ethics* (Oxford: Oxford University Press, 2002).

Boswell, James, *Life of Johnson* (Oxford: Oxford University Press, 1980).

Copi, Irving M., *Introduction to Logic* (London, Paris, New York: Pearson Education, 2009).

Cox, Gary, *How to be an Existentialist, or How to Get Real, Get a Grip and Stop Making Excuses* (London and New York: Continuum, 2009).

Descartes, René, *Discourse on Method and The Meditations*, trans. F. E. Sutcliffe (London: Penguin, 2007).

Gerrold, David, *Taking the Red Pill: Science Philosophy and Religion in The Matrix* (Camberwell: Penguin Australia, 2004).

Gray, Thomas, *Elegy Written in a Country Churchyard and Other Poems* (London: Penguin, 2009).

Hick, John H., *Philosophy of Religion* (Englewood Cliffs, NJ: Prentice-Hall, 1990).

Hodges, Wilfrid, *Logic* (London: Penguin, 2001).

Hume, David, *Enquiries Concerning Human Understanding and Concerning the Principles of Morals*, ed. L. A. Selby-Bigge (Oxford: Oxford University Press, 1975).

Hume David, *A Treatise of Human Nature*, ed. L. A. Selby-Bigge (Oxford: Oxford University Press, 1978).

Irwin, William, *The Matrix and Philosophy: Welcome to the Desert of the Real* (Chicago, IL: Open Court, 2002).

Kant, Immanuel, *Critique of Pure Reason*, trans. Norman Kemp Smith (London: Macmillan, 2003).

Kant, Immanuel, *Prolegomena to Any Future Metaphysics*, trans. Paul Carus (Indianapolis, IN: Hackett, 1983).

Keats, John, *The Complete Poems* (London: Penguin, 2003).

Mackie, J. L., *Ethics: Inventing Right and Wrong* (London: Penguin, 1990).

Mill, John Stuart, *On Liberty and Other Essays* (Oxford: Oxford University Press, 1998).

Monk, Ray, *Ludwig Wittgenstein: The Duty of Genius* (London: Vintage, 1991).

Nietzsche, Friedrich, *The Gay Science*, trans. Walter Kaufmann (New York: Vintage, 1974).

Nietzsche, Friedrich, *The Wanderer and his Shadow*, second supplement to *Human, All too Human*, trans. R. J. Hollingdale (Cambridge: Cambridge University Press, 1996).

O'Brien, Dan, *An Introduction to the Theory of Knowledge* (Cambridge: Polity Press, 2006).

Pirsig, Robert M., *Zen and the Art of Motorcycle Maintenance: An Inquiry into Values* (London and New York: Vintage, 1974).

Plato, *The Apology*, in *The Last Days of Socrates*, trans. Hugh Tredennick (London: Penguin, 2003).

Plato, *The Republic*, trans. Desmond Lee (London: Penguin, 2007).

Russell, Bertrand, *Human Knowledge: Its Scope and Limits* (London and New York: Routledge, 2009).

Russell, Bertrand, *In Praise of Idleness: And Other Essays* (London and New York: Routledge, 2004).

Russell, Bertrand, *Why I am Not a Christian: And Other Essays on Religion and Related Subjects* (London and New York: Routledge, 2004).

Sartre, Jean-Paul, *Being and Nothingness*: *An Essay on Phenomenological Ontology*, trans. Hazel E. Barnes (London and New York: Routledge, 2003).

Sartre, Jean-Paul, *The Imaginary: A Phenomenological Psychology of the Imagination*, trans. Jonathan Webber (London and New York: Routledge, 2004).

Swift, Jonathan, *Gulliver's Travels* (London: Penguin, 2003).

Thompson, Hunter S., *Fear and Loathing in Las Vegas: A Savage Journey to the Heart of the American Dream* (London: Harper Perennial, 2005).

Velecky, Lubor, 'The Five Ways: Proofs Of God's Existence?', in *Monist 58* (January 1974): pp. 38–51.

Whitehead, Alfred North, *Process and Reality* (New York: Macmillan, 1979).

Williams, Bernard, *Descartes: The Project of Pure Enquiry* (London: Penguin, 1990).

Wittgenstein, Ludwig, *Philosophical Investigations*, trans. G. E. M. Anscombe (Oxford: Blackwell, 1988).

Wittgenstein, Ludwig, *Tractatus Logico-Philosophicus*, trans. D. F. Pears and B. F. McGuiness (London and New York: Routledge, 2001).

Visual, Musical and Internet Media References

The Beatles, *Lucy in the Sky with Diamonds*, Track 3, *Sgt. Pepper's Lonely Hearts Club Band* (Parlophone, EMI, 1967).

British Philosophical Association Web Site: www.bpa.ac.uk

Family Guy: The Son Also Draws, Episode 6, Season 1 (20th Century Fox Home Entertainment, 2001).

The Matrix (Village Roadshow Pictures, Warner Brothers, 1999).

Monty Python's The Meaning of Life (Universal Studios, 1983).

Red Dwarf: Back to Reality, Episode 6, Series 5 (BBC Worldwide, 2004).

Further Reading

Baggini, Julian, *What's it All About?: Philosophy and the Meaning of Life* (London: Granta, 2005).

De Botton, Alain, *The Consolations of Philosophy* (London: Penguin, 2001).

Gaarder, Jostein, *Sophie's World: A Novel about the History of Philosophy*, trans. Paulette Moller (London: Phoenix, 1995).

Grayling, A. C., *The Meaning of Things: Applying Philosophy to Life* (London: Phoenix, 2002).

Hankinson, Jim, *Bluff Your Way in Philosophy* (Horsham: Ravette, 1994).

Russell, Bertrand, *History of Western Philosophy* (London and New York: Routledge, 2004).

Scruton, Roger, *Philosophy: Principles and Problems* (London and New York: Continuum, 2005).

Warburton, Nigel, *Philosophy: The Basics* (London and New York: Routledge, 2004).

Index